Feeling Stuck In Life

Breaking Free Brick By Brick

Dr. Christina Baker

Instagram: @merakijourney_therapy

Copyright © 2024 Dr. Christina Baker

All rights reserved.

ISBN: 9798340843722

DEDICATION
Defying Stagnation and Crafting a Dynamic Life

    To the beautiful souls who have supported me during my season of feeling stagnant and purposeless, thank you from the bottom of my heart. Thank you for your patience. Thank you for your constant encouragements. Thank you for your gentle nudge every once in a while. And thank you for consistently considering my mental wellbeing.

    I am deeply grateful for your presence in my life, and the positive impact you've had on my journey. Your steadfast support has kept me anchored, and provided me with the grace that I needed. Your kindness and understanding made my season of stagnation both bearable and rewarding.

    I am truly fortunate to have you by my side. Your unwavering support not only helped me to navigate my challenges, but also empowered me to grow and share my insights with others. Together, we've turned a difficult season into an opportunity for growth, learning, and prosperity. For this, I will always appreciate and value you. Forever Grateful.

Yours Truly,

Dr. Christina Baker

BREAKING THROUGH BRICK BY BRICK

TABLE OF CONTENTS

Acknowledgments   i

Part 1: We're All in This Together   1
Exploring the Common Grounds of Feeling Stagnant

Part 2: Understanding Stagnation
Complexities of Feeling Stuck in Life   30

Part 3: The Center of it All   54
Digging Deeper: Uncovering the Roots of Stagnation

Part 4: Construct Your Path
Breaking Through Brick by Brick   113

Part 5: The Phoenix Method
Unshackled by the Past   118

Author's Message   127

Book Cover: Ricardo Reid

BREAKING THROUGH BRICK BY BRICK

MERAKI JOURNEY FAMILY:

Thank you for being a part of the Meraki Journey Family. Your continued support will always be genuinely appreciated. As always, the Meraki Journey Family is committed to cultivating independent thinking, and leveraging tools that best serve our needs. With that being said, on this Meraki Journey of pushing past stagnation, we will focus on mental instabilities, uncovering the root causes of stagnation, exploring the common grounds of stagnation, and navigating a stagnant prone society.

Similar to "Meraki Journey: Transitioning from a Liability to an Asset", this book will highlight unpopular and unconventional practices that will defy stagnation. We seek to break generational curses, generational patterns, and to learn from our own mistakes, and the mistakes of others. Instead of relying on what's trendy and praised by the masses, let's become innovative and creative with our solutions.

Note: Remember, although our Meraki Journey may complement or enhance religious or spiritual beliefs, it is not meant to replace them.

Thank You,

Meraki Journey Team
Instagram: @merakijourney_therapy

Graceful Readers,

This self-help guide is thoughtfully designed to support your unique journey of growth and healing. Each chapter addresses challenges that can leave you feeling stuck—whether they arise in your professional life, emotional well-being, spiritual path, personal relationships, environment, mental habits, or daily routines.

As you read through this book, you'll come across several unconventional ways to heal from past trauma—with one being "The Phoenix Method". Please be aware that this method may resonate with each reader differently; however, I encourage you to follow the book step by step.

Each chapter builds on the last, helping you to better understand this powerful technique when you reach it. Please remember that healing isn't a one-size-fits-all process. The Meraki Journey team has made every effort to offer guidance that speaks to a wide range of experiences and struggles.

We sincerely hope that no matter which part of this book you connect with, it helps you to break free from anything that may be holding you back. Thank you for your trust and continued support. May this book inspire new heights of freedom, growth, and fulfillment in your life.

Wishing you strength and success on your journey forward.

- **Meraki Journey Therapy**

Part 1: We're All in This Together
Exploring the Common Grounds of Feeling Stuck

You know that feeling you get in the pit of your soul when:

- Rejection seems to be a recurring theme?
- Finding your purpose in life becomes a discouraging experience?
- Progress and advancement seem to avoid you, regardless of your efforts?
- You feel trapped between a 'rock and a hard place'?
- Your options feel limited and constrained?
- It always feels like there's a piece of the puzzle is missing from your life?

Chances are, you may be experiencing stagnation in one or more areas of your life. And trust me, we've all experienced a version of it—though our outcomes and reasons for it may not be the same.

A. Some may only experience this feeling briefly during different phases of their lives.

B. While the rest of us may find ourselves in prolonged states of stagnation. This level of stagnancy often shapes our identity, and alters our perception of reality.

Nevertheless, *how* we respond to stagnation is crucial to our mental wellbeing, our journey towards self-betterment, and a life filled with joyous experiences.

From an early age, I meticulously created a thoughted out plan—detailing how I would one day earn a PhD, own a big house, have a great husband, and create my own loving family. *I didn't know it back then, but I have come to realize that my plan was dangerous.* Although having goals and desires served me well, I didn't prepare myself for all the pivots, changes, struggles, rejections, and the rollercoaster types of relationships I'd experience along the way.

At the time, I was too inexperience to account for all the distractions, delays, sabotages, emotional and spiritual battles I'd eventually endure. Needless to say, when these moments did come, I wasn't prepare for any of it. For a very long time, whenever life would throw me a curve ball I would either panic, have a mental breakdown, or kept myself stuck in a mindset of *why isn't anything going my way—no matter how hard I try?*

I was so goal-oriented and driven, that I failed to appreciate how beautiful life truly is. Instead of taking the time to acknowledge and celebrate my *small* accomplishments, my strict nature of wanting to achieve bigger milestones was in control. I feared being left behind by my peers, and felt the need to prove my worthiness of love and approval from my *family*. So much so, that I pushed myself relentlessly.

Now that have a healthier mindset, I am aware that my overachieving nature was a danger to my happiness and mental wellbeing. My unhealed mindset and behavior were the chief ambassadors to my stagnation, and sense of defeat. Yes, I've earned my degrees—which I am proud and grateful for. Yes, I am a published author—which I am also proud of. And yes, I have also successfully checked off numerous accomplishments from my list. *The same list that I have revised countless times over the decades.*

But yet still, I found myself in a mindset of stagnation. Instead of celebrating my accomplishments, I've been stuck—trapped in past hurts and letdowns. I've been frustrated by the reality of not being where, and who I've convinced myself I needed to be by this time. But why is that? Why do I feel this way? Why am I struggling with my emotions? Why do I feel so unsuccessful? Why do I sometimes lack the strength to keep depression at bay? Why do *I* feel stuck?

Through years of introspection and seeking answers to my questions, I've learned some hard truths. I've learned that for way too long, I have allowed my happiness to be:

- Contingent on if my family is proud of me or not.
- Reliant on a timeline that I've created for my accomplishments.
- Dictated by societal expectations of me.
- Controlled by external factors that I have no control over.

Dr. Christina Baker

Stagnation Isn't a Respecter of Persons

Whether successful or financially unstable, surrounded by love or completely isolated—stagnation doesn't discriminate. So, since we're all in this together, let's agree that on a few things:

1. Feeling stuck or overwhelmed in one area of our lives shouldn't overshadow the joy, gratitude, or excitement we can experience in other areas of our lives.

2. Stagnation is a mental prison, but the good news is that we hold the key to our own liberations.

3. The feeling of being stuck might be a misinterpretation. In some cases, what we truly need is a moment to pause and self-reflect.

4. Stagnation shouldn't defined our worth or our levels of success. It's a temporary state of mind, not a reflection of our true potential and capabilities.

5. Stagnation is a deceptive comfort that makes us reluctant to break free from familiarity and unproductive routines.

6. Stagnation can serve as a catalyst for unexpected opportunities—if we allow it to inspire us to reevaluate our goals, plans, reactions, and thought processes.

7. Stagnation is **not** failure; it's an indication that growth is needed. By embracing it, we can shift our perspectives and take deliberate steps toward transformation and progress.

<u>Trapped in Anxiety:</u> *How I got out*

Am I the only one who dreads hearing: *"if you feel so stuck in life, why don't you just get up and do something about it?"*

Feeling stuck or stagnant is a complex experience that can leave us struggling to articulate our emotions. We may cry out for help, either loudly or silently. In my case, I did both. I recognized that I needed support to escape the depression stemming from my stagnation. However, what I found most challenging was expressing my feelings to others, and conveying how they could help me during this difficult season of stagnancy.

The Art of Intentionality Vs. Impact

Feeling Stuck	**Loved Ones**
If you find yourself struggling with stagnation, and feel that you lack support, take a moment to self-reflect before speaking. Always remember that, <u>***how***</u> you ask for help may be even more important than asking for help itself.	If you are a loved one of someone who is struggling with stagnation, offering genuine <u>***understanding***</u> and *empathy* can significantly help them overcome the hurdles of feeling stuck.

Missing The Signs
Ineffective Communication

      It's easy for an **outsider** to miss the signs of a cry for help. But it's even easier to miss the signs when the **insider** doesn't even have a clear understanding of what they're experiencing. Feeling stuck in a certain area of life can lead to symptoms of depression, and various forms of paralysis.

The lack of understanding can cause frustration, isolation, and confusion for everyone involved, as the experience of stagnation can look very different for those on the inside than those observing from the outside.

Insiders May Feel	**Outsiders May See**
Misunderstood	Procrastination
Abandon	Laziness
Paranoid	Moodiness
Depressed	Unexplained isolation
Fear	Low self-esteem
Rejected	Poor sense of self-worth
Paralysis	Unwarranted frustration or anger
Clouded or Heavy	No motivation/determination
Shame	Self-Victimization
Unworthy	Poor sense of self

How to Communicate in these moments?

In order to communicate effectively in moments of stagnation, both sides have to respect the fact that their perception of the situation may be different. Regardless of the differences, no one's reality is **more** real or **truer** than the other. Therefore, instead of judging, or going back and forth about what is *real* and what is not, or what makes sense and what does not, let's practice positive communication with each other.

Here are some examples of how you (insider) can effectively communicate with loved ones (outsider).

- "I've been feeling a bit stuck lately, and I could use some guidance. Would you mind listening and offering your perspective?"

- "I'm struggling with motivation and a sense of direction. Can we talk about it, and maybe you can share your thoughts on how to move forward?"

- "I'm feeling stuck, and I'm not sure how to break out of it. Your advice or support would mean a lot to me."

- "I'm going through a phase of stagnation, and I'm open to suggestions. Have you ever faced something similar, if so, how did you overcome it?"

- "I need help navigating this feeling of being stuck. Can we brainstorm together, or explore potential solutions that could work for me?"

Here are some examples of how loved ones (outsider) can effectively communicate with you (insider).

- "I understand and respect how you feel, what can I do to eliminate or reduce that experience for you?"

- "Although it wasn't my intention to hurt you, I understand the impact my actions and words have caused you."

- "How can I best support you in this time of stagnation?"

- "What specific aspect of your life is contributing to this sense of feeling suck?"

- "What specific things can I do to show my support in a positive way?"

Chrissy's Journal Entry:

No Sense of Self

...*Once you allow stagnation's grip to tighten over time, deterioration in the mind starts to set in—clouding your thoughts, and breaking down your will to do anything productive. Then suddenly a subtle competition between your physical and mental well-being emerges.*

It's like quicksand, the longer you stay stuck—the harder it is to fight your way out of it. Before you know it, you're covered and consumed by worry, frustration, anxiety, what ifs, and so much more.

It's like you're in a tunnel, but there's no light. And there's no end. It's like nothing else matters—not what came before, nor what will come after. All you know is that you're in darkness, with:

- → *No sense of time—time of when things will change.*
- → *No sense place—where you stand in people's lives.*
- → *No sense of direction—where do you go from here?*
- → *No sense of hope—you're stuck, no one cares, and no one understands.*
- → *No sense of self—it's almost inevitable to lose yourself in such darkness.*

Finding Strength In Community

From a very young age, I've always found solace in documenting my emotions and experiences. However, that's usually the furthest I'd go. I wouldn't normally seek any solutions or help for anything that have been through. In a way, I thought that expressing myself and experiencing a sense of release was all that I needed to move forward. Fortunately, as time progressed, I've learned that there's strength in having a healthy community around me.

Yes, it's true that journaling:

- Provokes self-reflection.
- Enhances emotional intelligence.
- Represents a sacred and safe space.
- Provides insight into our experiences.
- Uncover patterns in our thinking.
- Serves as a therapeutic practice that aids in
    - Stress management
    - Goal setting
    - Maintaining an overall healthy mindset.

But is it enough? If we want to be free from the thickening quicksand of stagnation, we will need go a step further.

Note: While self-help is the core of the Meraki Journey, no one can thrive in isolation. So, let's discover how to seek positive external support.

Seeking Positive External Support

There are two key reasons why seeking positive external support can be challenging:

- **Self-Sabotage:** Past traumas, lack of self-awareness, or a combination of bad habits can lead us to seek comfort in unhealthy forms of support.
- **Self-Doubt:** Feelings of shame, mistrust, and fear can become barriers to our healing and growth. Never allow these emotions to overshadow your desire to heal and progress.

Acknowledging our vulnerabilities and allowing ourselves to receive help is a courageous act that can lead to profound transformation. Therefore, before seeking external support, it's important to go through several phrases of positive self-transformation.

Note: Positive self-transformation will cause us to develop wisdom, discipline, and discernment—qualities that guides us in knowing *when* and *whom* to open up to.

Whether through therapy, loved ones, or our community, **positive external support** can:

⇒ Provide fresh perspectives.

⇒ Equip us with valuable tools to overcome stagnation and trauma.

⇒ Highlights the value of meaningful connections.

⇒ Remind us that we're not alone in our experiences.

Case Illustration:

Before breaking down the four types of external support, allow me to illustrate the risks associated with <u>solely</u> depending on your own knowledge and understandings.

Let's take a skilled driver for example:

1. She has memorized most of the road laws and guidelines.
2. She knows every pothole, twist, and turn on her daily routes to work, loved ones' homes, and favorite restaurants.
3. She can describe in detail every car she has driven up until today.
4. She even has the ability to fix her own car whenever there's an issue.

Illustration Questions:

1. Does this mean that she doesn't need assistance from her rearview mirror, side mirrors, traffic lights, and the indication from other vehicles?
2. Does this mean that using the GPS, back up camera, and car sensors wouldn't make her journey easier?
3. Does this mean that she shouldn't consider exploring alternative routes to her destinations in case of accidents or roadblocks?

Note: Even with experience and knowledge, external support can provide clarity, ease, and new possibilities— just like in life. So, let's normalize seeking support **even** if we feel like we can *make it through* just fine on our own.

Illustration Assessment:

Seeking support shouldn't be reserved for when we are overwhelmed, ran out of options, or on the verge of giving up. Seeking support should be woven into our everyday lives.

- Sometimes, we may just need our journey to be a little easier.

- Sometimes, we may just need our load to feel a little lighter.

- Sometimes, we may lose our way, and simply need help finding the path again.

- Sometimes, we may just need someone by our side to keep us awake and motivated along the way.

- Sometimes, we may just need a friend's comforting presence to remind us that we aren't alone.

- Sometimes, we may just need to be reminded that we are heard, loved, seen, cared for, supported, and understood.

Note: Stagnation, trauma, life's ups and downs, and relationship challenges don't discriminate. Therefore, support is for <u>everyone</u>, and in <u>any</u> season of our lives.

Let's talk about it !

Here are four types of external support:

> **1. Mentor:** A Guiding Light in Our Journey
> Mentors empower us with the <u>evidence of **their own**</u> success. Their purpose is to provide wisdom and suggestions that can aid in dealing with our situations.

Type of Stagnation: Mentorship is well-suited for addressing stagnation related to career development, skill enhancement, or navigating specific professional challenges. A mentor can offer guidance and insights to help us to overcome obstacles, set and achieve goals, and advance in our careers.

Note: Learn from your mentors' successes and failures. But keep in mind that, *what worked for them may not work for you*—vice versa.

> **2. Coach:** Recognizing Potential & Encouraging Success
> Coaches empower us to find **our own** solutions by maximizing on our true potentials.

Type of Stagnation: Coaching is suitable for addressing stagnation related to personal growth, goal-setting, enhancing skills, and make significant life changes.

1. Anyone can be a coach in your life. However, it is important to make sure that the coaching you are receiving aligns with your core believes and values.

2. Be careful that you aren't allowing anyone to <u>project their desires</u> onto you. Remember that your limit may not be the same as your coaches' limits—vice versa.

3. Therapy: Nurturing Mental & Emotional Well-Being. It is absolutely important to have stable and consistent emotional support. Therapists provides a safe space for us to explore and process our emotions.

Type of Stagnation: Therapy is best suited to address stagnation related to mental health issues, emotional challenges, and unresolved psychological issues. Therapists help with exploring underlying factors that contribute to stagnation, address negative thought patterns, manage stress, and develop coping strategies.

4. Community: Enhancing Interpersonal Skills. Community support can:

- Boost your social confidence.
- Reduce isolation.
- Improve your communication skills.
- Enhance your conflict resolution skills.
- Improve your relationship-building skills.

Note: The "every man for themselves" mentality, can cause an entire community of people to struggle with the same issues—*alone*. Causing us to feel unmotivated, defeated, and isolated.

Type of Stagnation: Community support is best suited to address stagnation related to creative blockage, professional plateauing, and emotional burnout.

Note: Yes, community support can help with loneliness and isolation. However, be careful not to trauma bond.

Expanding Your Support Options

There's no need to box yourself in or limit your options. It's possible for you to require multiple forms of support for one or more areas of your life at the same time. Just as you may experience stagnation in different aspects of your life, you may also need a variety of resources to address these challenges. To better understand which type of support you need for your unique situation, ask yourself these guiding questions:

- What area in my life am I experiencing stagnation?
- What type of stagnation am I dealing with?
- What type of support do I believe would be most beneficial for me?
    - Mentorship, Community support, Therapy, or Coaching?
- Why do I believe that this option is the best fit for my experience?
- What has prevented me from seeking support in the past?
- What specific goals do I want to achieve through seeking support?

**For more information on seeking the right support that is tailored to your needs and style, please visit Meraki Journey Therapy at @merakijourney_therapy on Instagram or at www.merakijourneytherapy.com. Meraki Journey Therapy is designed to revolutionize the way we access support. We encourage growth and aid in healing by offering guidance, resources, and therapy along the way.

I Owe It To My Mentor

For a long time, I felt trapped in my career, stuck in a cycle of frustration and stagnation. Promotions seemed out of reach, and my dissatisfaction only deepened when my family began pressuring me about buying a house and starting a family. The weight of their expectations became overwhelming, and I found myself longing to disappear—if only for a little while—to find some peace and hear my own thoughts.

After years of feeling lost and unfulfilled, I knew I needed guidance. That's when I reached out to a mentor. Their support changed everything. With their help, I gained clarity on my goals, identified areas where I could grow, and developed a concrete plan to move forward. Together, we explored new opportunities, and I acquired valuable skills that reignited my passion.

Reaching out for support was one of the best decisions I ever made. It not only helped me break free from my stagnant state, but it also paved the way for profound personal and professional growth. I now feel empowered to pursue the life I truly want.

-Rachel Winters

Part 2: Understanding Stagnation
The Complexities of Feeling Stuck in Life

Why does it seem as though stagnation is effecting more and more people each day? Why is stagnation becoming so prevalent, despite the fact that we have more options and choices available to us than ever before? In this book we will discuss unconventional factors that contributes to a sense of stagnation for many of us—despite having a plethora of opportunities at our fingertips.

By pinpointing specific causes of stagnation in our lives, we can give ourselves the opportunity to practice better habits, and strategies to avoid repeating the same mistakes. For instance, if decision paralysis is an issue for you, practicing decision-making techniques or simplifying your choices can help in breaking free from stagnation.

Choice-Based Stagnation:

- **Decision Paralysis:** Having an abundance of choices can be overwhelming, leading to a state of indecision. *Too many options can lead to zero decisions made.*
- **Toxic Achievement Culture:** Society often pressures individuals to quickly achieve specific milestones and successes—causing stress and a sense of stagnancy when these expectations aren't met.
- **Technological Distractions:** While technology provides endless information and connection, it also brings constant distractions. Social media in particular can lead to procrastination and unhealthy comparisons, which further fuel feelings of stagnation.

Solutions and activities for all topics can be found in our guided self-help journal, *Navigating Stagnation: Strategic Journaling*. This journal is the perfect tool to help you apply the skills and insights gained through the discussions in this book.

Navigating Stagnation: Strategic Journaling is a valuable resource because it:

- ♥ Provides structured prompts to help you reflect on your personal and professional growth.

- ♥ Encourages self-awareness and accountability in overcoming stagnation.

- ♥ Offers practical exercises to solidify your learning and implement real-life strategies.

- ♥ Allows you to track your progress and see tangible improvements over time.

Now, let's dive back into the many more topics of stagnation. Happy learning, healing, progressing, and thriving!

The Influences and Effects of Personality Styles

When it comes to feeling stuck, our personality traits and habits play a significant role. By understanding the influences that lead to stagnation, and the effects that follow, we can further break free from the cycle.

Influences: Potential causes of stagnation

- **Procrastination:** When we constantly put off tasks, we fall into a cycle of inaction.
- **Avoidance of Change:** Fear of the unknown can make us resist the very changes that we may need to grow.
- **Self-Doubt:** Hesitating to take risks or pursue new opportunities can cause us to remain in the same place.
- **Lack of Clear Goals:** A lack of direction can result in aimlessness and stagnation.
- **Perfectionism:** Striving for perfection can also lead to paralysis. When we fear making mistakes, we often avoid action altogether.

Effects: Potential effects of stagnation

- **Psychological Impact:** When we're stuck in a rut, feelings of boredom and dissatisfaction start to take over, making it harder to find joy in our daily lives.
- **Unwilling to learn new things:** When we stop seeking growth, we limit our potential.
- **Trapped in our comfort zone:** When we feel stuck, we become even more attached to what's familiar, making it difficult to push past our boundaries and limitations.

How We React to Stagnation Matters: While understanding the causes of stagnation provides insight, the way we respond is even more crucial because it directly shapes our outcomes. The truth is, we can't always control the circumstances that causes us to feel stuck, but we can control how we choose to navigate through them. Therefore, instead of viewing stagnation as a dead end, we can choose to see it as a powerful signal to adjust a few things, or to grow in certain areas of our lives.

Here are two personality styles that illustrates how we perceive and respond to stagnation.

Personality Styles	Perceptions of Stagnation	Typical Responses
1. Resilient and optimistic	Define stagnation as a temporary setback.	Actively seek solutions and opportunities for growth.
2. Defeatist and pessimistic	Define stagnation as a permanent hinderance.	Feel overwhelmed or stuck in a stagnant situation.
1. Adaptable and proactive	Define stagnation as a challenge to overcome.	Change or adjust approaches and habits to overcome stagnation.
2. Passive and comfort-seeking	Define stagnation as uncomfortable.	Resist breaking out of established patterns.
1. Open-minded and curious	Define stagnation as a prompt for discovery and self-betterment.	Take initiative in pursing new experiences and opportunities for improvement.
2. Fear of failure and change	Define stagnation as intimidating.	Prioritize comfort over growth.

-Created by Dr. Baker

Trait Spectrum
4 Traits: *Two Opposing Extremes*

Let's take a look at 4 different traits—ranging between their two opposing extremes.

As you learn about each trait and its opposing extremes, consider asking yourself the following questions to determine whether your traits are currently serving you well, or if they are contributing to life's challenges, such as stagnation.

1. Where do I fall on each trait spectrum when I am feeling stagnant?
2. Are my traits working out for me, or am I struggling *because* of them?
3. How do my current traits influence my approach to overcome stagnation?
4. How does each trait affect my emotions during moments of stagnancy?
5. Which traits are best for me when trying to break out of a stagnant phase?
6. Are there specific traits that I should develop or strengthen to better navigate through these phases?

Note: Please keep in mind that we are solely focusing on the opposing extremes of each trait. Therefore, it is more than likely that you may find yourself relating to each trait at varying degrees.

1.   *A* ←←← **Openness to Experiences** →→→ *B*

<u>A:</u> Seeks newness and change when dealing with stagnation

- Engages in diverse hobbies and interests.
- Enjoys brainstorming and creative projects.
- Seeks out educational opportunities.
- Adapts to dynamic environments.
- Embraces change and *uncertainty*.

<u>B:</u> Sticks to routine and familiarity when dealing with stagnation.

- Prefers established routines and activities.
- Sticks with familiar hobbies and interests.
- Follows a <u>set</u> career path.
- Prefers structure and order.
- Refines and perfects *existing* skills.

2.   *A* ←←← **Conscientiousness** →→→ *B*

<u>A:</u> Better equipped to manage stagnation by setting clear goals and developing plans to overcome obstacles.

- Highly organized and dependable
- Sets high standards.
- Disciplined and committed.
- Values punctuality and reliability.
- Efficient and effective in task completion.

<u>B:</u> Typically struggle more with stagnation due to a lack of direction and motivation.

- Spontaneous and flexible.
- May struggle with organization.
- Enjoys creativity and improvisation.
- Values freedom.
- Adapts to changing circumstances.

3.   *A* ←←← <u>**Agreeableness**</u> →→→ *B*

<u>*A:*</u> More inclined to seek support from others and collaborate on finding solutions to stagnant situations.

- Highly cooperative.
- Prioritizes others' needs.
- Empathetic and compassionate.
- Trusts others easily.
- Enjoys helping others.

<u>*B:*</u> Struggles to form and maintain positive relationships—limiting social support and resources.

- Self-focused.
- Engages in conflict if needed.
- Appears critical or skeptical.
- Values independence.
- Focuses on <u>personal</u> successes.

4.   *A* ←←← <u>**Neuroticism**</u> →→→ *B*

<u>*A:*</u> Prone to anxiety, depression, and stress—often feels overwhelmed in stagnant situations.

- Experiences frequent mood swings.
- Highly sensitive to criticism.
- Struggles with uncertainty.
- Experiences self-doubt.
- Highly empathetic to others' emotions.

<u>*B:*</u> Resilient and practices positive coping strategies when feeling stagnant.

- Maintains a calm and stable mood.
- Less affected by criticism.
- Copes well with uncertainty.
- Realist: Maintains a <u>balanced</u> perspective.
- Rarely feels intense negative emotions.

Self-Check-In Questions

After understanding how specific personality traits impact your response to stagnation, ask yourself a series of self-check-in questions:

1. What does my reaction to stagnation reveals about my personality traits?
2. What have I learned about myself while going through the trait spectrum?
3. What are some coping mechanisms for when I am feeling stuck or stagnant?
4. What is my typical thought pattern when experiencing stagnation?
5. What actions should I take to overcome stagnation?
6. Is there anything that I need change or explore more about myself?
7. How should I respond to hardships?
8. How can I maintain motivation and momentum when faced with stagnancy?
9. What strategies can I use to overcome the challenges associated with stagnation?
10. Why is self-pity so dangerous in my life's journey?

Note: By examining how our personality traits interact with stagnation, we can incorporate more effective coping mechanisms, increase self-awareness, and better understand how our traits influence our experiences.

Empowered Mindset vs. Victim Mentality

Changing your mindset will change your life's experience.

The difference between an empowered mindset and a victim mentality lies in how we <u>perceive</u> and <u>respond</u> to challenges and obstacles.

- **<u>Empowered mindset</u> (*Action*):** Takes ownership of our situation, and actively seek to overcome stagnation.
- **<u>Victim mentality</u> (*Emotion*):** Feels powerless when experiencing stagnation.

Here are 5 examples:

1. Perception of Control:

◊ **Empowered Mindset:** Believes in having control and influence over our circumstances and outcomes. Usually sees challenges as opportunities for growth and progress.

◊ **Victim Mentality:** Believes that <u>external</u> factors dictate their lives. Often viewing themselves as victims of their circumstances—leading to a sense of <u>helplessness, hopelessness,</u> and blind <u>acceptance.</u>

2. Response to Stagnation:

◊ **Empowered Mindset:** Actively seeks ways to break free by setting goals, finding resources, and taking actions to move forward.

◊ **Victim Mentality:** Believes that nothing they do will make a difference; and blames <u>others</u> or <u>external</u> conditions for their lack of progress.

3. Emotional Impact:

- ◊ **Empowered Mindset:** Exudes confidence, self-assurance, control, and motivation. Usually experience <u>higher</u> self-esteem and self-worth, while experiencing <u>lower</u> levels of stress and dissatisfaction.

- ◊ **Victim Mentality:** Generates feelings of frustration, powerlessness, irritation, and resentment. Usually experience <u>lower</u> self-esteem and self-worth, while experiencing <u>higher</u> levels of stress and dissatisfaction.

4. Perspective on Failure:

- ◊ **Empowered Mindset:** Views failure as a valuable learning experience, and uses it to improve skills and strategies.

- ◊ **Victim Mentality:** Sees failure as <u>confirmation</u> of inadequacy. Often avoid risks and opportunities due to fear of repeating past mistakes, which reinforces a cycle of inaction.

5. Problem-Solving Approach:

- ◊ **Empowered Mindset:** Embraces a proactive approach to problem-solving. Views obstacles as challenges to be tackled resourcefully and wise.

- ◊ **Victim Mentality:** Tends to avoid addressing problems. Often feels overwhelmed—resorting to denial or blame.

Transitioning from a **victim mentality** to an **empowered mindset** in just <u>four</u> steps. **B. E. S. T.:**

- ⇒ **B**ecome Self-Aware
- ⇒ **E**xercise Inward Positivity
- ⇒ **S**hift Your Perspective
- ⇒ **T**ransform Your Words

1. Become Self-Aware:

Self-awareness enables us to gain a deeper understanding of our thoughts, feelings, motivations, traits, and behaviors.

It helps us to:

- * Improve our decision-making skills.
- * Manage our emotions.
- * Build stronger relationships.
- * Enhance our resilience.
- * Achieve self-improvement.

When we are more self-aware, it becomes easier to identify and overcome **limited beliefs**.

Limited beliefs are negative thoughts that holds us back from achieving our goals, and keep us stuck in our comfort zones. These types of beliefs often stems from past experiences, societal influences, and self-doubt. Limited beliefs can lead to self-sabotage, procrastination, and missed opportunities.

Example of limited beliefs: **"I'll never be able to do that"**: Assuming certain challenges are beyond your capabilities.

2. Exercise Inward Positivity:

Practice unconditional gratitude by focusing on what you have rather than what you lack. This approach doesn't dismiss our feelings or experiences; instead, it help us to prevent negative thoughts from overshadowing the positive aspects of our lives.

1. Acknowledge your struggles with compassion, and avoid harsh self-judgments.
2. Transform <u>destructive</u> thinking into <u>constructive</u> thinking for a more empowering mindset.

Constructive Thinking Vs. Destructive Thinking

- <u>Constructive Thinking</u>: Allows us to focus our energy and resources on finding solutions, learning from mistakes, and seeing challenges as opportunities for <u>growth</u>.
- <u>Destructive Thinking:</u> Traps us in a cycle of focusing on problems without pursuing solutions. It leads us to view challenges as unmanageable and reinforces a negative, pessimistic mindset.

Constructive	Destructive
This is a great opportunity to find innovative solutions.	I will never succeed.
What can I learn from this experience for next time?	This is a disaster; I'll never get it right.

3. Shift Your Perspective:

Positive Perspective: Focuses on opportunities and strengths. Encourages optimism and resilience.	**Negative Perspective:** Focuses on limitations and failures. Pessimistic and discouraging.
Constructive Thinking: Engages in solution-oriented thoughts that promotes growth and improvement.	**Destructive Thinking:** Engages in self-defeating thoughts that hinder progress and reinforce negative beliefs.
Problem-Solving Mindset: Actively seeks solutions and alternatives. Fosters adaptability and creativity.	**A Sense of Hopelessness:** Feels trapped and overwhelmed. Experiences inaction and despair.

Shifting Your Perspective:

- **Challenge Negative Thoughts:** Each day for 30 days, consciously speak the opposite of your negative beliefs about yourself—along with behaving as though it is true.

- **Journaling for Growth:** Each week, document any changes or progress in your mindset and self-esteem.

**Continue the 'shifting your perspective' exercise in your Navigating Stagnation: Strategic Journaling journal.

4. Transform Your Words:

It's essential to be mindful of the words you use to describe yourself and your experiences. Always remember that your words are powerful enough to shape your perspective, and impact how you operate in the world.

Here are a few examples of **Intentional Speaking**:

Stagnant Speaking	Intentional Speaking
I'm not good enough.	I am capable of success.
I'll never be as good as others.	I acknowledge my progress and celebrate my individuality.
I'm always so unlucky.	I create my own opportunities through hard work and positivity.
I'm constantly criticized.	I embrace constructive feedback and use it to grow.
I'm a failure.	I learn from setbacks and grow stronger.
Nobody cares about me.	I am surrounded by people who love and support me.
I'm not smart enough.	I have the ability to learn and adapt.
I'm too old/young.	My age brings unique experiences and perspectives.
I'm always overlooked.	I possess unique talents and qualities that will be recognized.
I'll never succeed.	I am determined to achieve my goals.

Stagnant Speaking Fuels Negative Self-Perception

Transforming the way we describe ourselves and our experiences, especially when discussing stagnation is important because it allows us to articulate our feelings more effectively. Making it easier for loved ones and other support systems to understand what we're truly going through.

When negative self-perception starts to creep in, ask yourself:

1. Are my thoughts supported by <u>factual</u> evidence?
2. Are they distracting me from pursuing what truly matters?
3. Are they dependent on my mood or current circumstances?
4. Are they rooted in unrealistic expectations?
5. Are they influenced by comparisons with others?
6. Are they contributing to my overall well-being?
7. Are they hindering my personal growth?

When to use <u>positive replacement</u> vs. when to use <u>intentional speaking</u>?

Let's Talk About It!

1. Use **Intentional Speaking** when you want to consciously frame your words and thoughts to reflect a desired outcome or mindset. It's about speaking with purpose and clarity, often to motivate, inspire, or guide yourself toward a specific goal. <u>This technique works well when you need to be deliberate in shaping your narrative,</u> and staying focused on the positive changes you're aiming to create.

2. Use **Positive Replacement Talk** when you're trying to counterbalance negative self-perceptions without directly opposing them. It's most helpful when you need to acknowledge both your strengths and weaknesses; reminding yourself that even if you're struggling in one area, you still have valuable qualities. <u>This approach is useful when you want to be **kinder** to yourself, and shift your focus to more balanced thinking.</u>

Remember, No one is perfect.

Balance your <u>self-awareness</u> with your <u>self-compassion</u>.

Here are a few examples of <u>Positive Replacements</u>:

Negative Traits	**Positive Replacements**
I often procrastinate.	I am incredibly, creative and resourceful.
I am terrible at public speaking.	I excel at problem-solving.
I sometimes doubt myself.	I am an amazing friend.
I sometimes find it hard to say no to others.	I am very organized and hardworking.
I sometimes worry too much about the future.	I am resilient and can adapt to challenges with grace.
I'm not as outgoing as I'd like to be.	I am a prolific writer.

How is this chart helpful—especially if it doesn't give a <u>direct solution</u> to the negative thoughts in our heads?

For example:

I'm not as outgoing as I'd like to be.	I am a prolific writer.

If I tried to change this truth about myself to "rewrite" my negative self-perceptions, I wouldn't truly be practicing honesty. Instead, I'd be:

- Trying to speak things into existence.
- Affirming myself.
- Willfully ignoring my self-awareness.

While speaking things into existence or affirming ourselves can be helpful, these approaches aren't always effective or appropriate during certain seasons of our lives.

In a season of stagnation, would it benefit you to *speak things into existence*, instead of being gracefully honest?

For example:

| I sometimes doubt myself. | I do **not** doubt myself. |

How will this kind of replacement help you in finding real solutions? This approach can be dangerous because it can easily lead to:

- **Diluted Feelings:** Prevention of addressing core issues.
- **Delusion:** Creation of a false sense of security by ignoring challenges.
- **Toxic Positivity:** Focus solely on positive thoughts while dismissing negative emotions. In other words, invalidating your own experiences.

Note: Positive replacement helps to keep us balanced, and away from sinking into depression or self-hate. It's important to learn when to use affirming techniques, and when to use positive replacements talk.

Addressing The Problem

Ignoring your negative qualities is just as detrimental as highlighting them.

1. Acknowledge negative qualities.
2. Practice Positive Replacement.
3. Address your negative traits directly.

Although not always the case, positive replacement can sometimes serve as a valuable tool we use to address our negative traits.

For example:

I sometimes worry too much about the future.	I am resilient and can adapt to challenges with grace.

While it's true that I often worry about what lies ahead, it's equally true that I am resilient and adaptable. By reminding myself of this positive truth, I reassure myself that no matter what challenges arise in the near or far future, I will handle them with grace. <u>Trusting in my resilience and adaptability calms my worries.</u>

Without highlighting this positive aspect, I might not have connected these two truths during moments of anxiety and despair. But what happens when our positive replacement isn't aligned enough to address a negative quality?

Complete 'addressing negative qualities' in your **<u>Navigating Stagnation: Strategic Journaling</u> to answer this question.

Breaking Free From Old Patterns:

In the journey of life, one of the greatest barriers we face is the reluctance to let go of old patterns that no longer serve us. The mindset of **"if it ain't broke, don't try to fix it"** can trap you in a stagnant lifestyle, confining us to a prison of outdated beliefs and limited potential for growth.

Here are a few more limiting mantras:

- → Same ole' same ole'
- → I am the way I am.
- → Can't teach an old dog new tricks.
- → I'm this way because of…

These phrases are not just expressions; they are shackles that bind you to a static existence. A motivational speaker once said, "One of the scariest things is the unwillingness to learn, even at your own expense". <u>Choosing</u> to remain stuck in old habits is not just irresponsible; it stifles your personal and professional growth. When we refuse to embrace change, we remain trapped in a narrow worldview, blinding ourselves to the richness of diverse perspectives.

This type of stubbornness to evolve and grow mentally can cause self-righteous behaviors, and the unwillingness to mature mentally, spiritually, and emotionally.

Dare to learn, unlearn, and relearn—your journey awaits.

-Meraki Journey Therapy

During my season of stagnation, I've experienced several concepts that has required me to **unlearn** or **relearn** a few things.

Here are 4 of them:

1. **Life Isn't Always Personal:** Not every challenge we face is a reflection of our own lives. Often, our discomforts are nudging us to seek solutions—not just for ourselves, but for others. *Embracing this perspective can deepen our compassion and empathy.*

2. **Rejection Holds Valuable Lessons:** Pay closer attention to your rejections than to your acceptances. Each "no" carries insights that can illuminate areas for improvement, highlight blind spots, and uncover growth opportunities. It can help us to learn from our mistakes, improve our approaches, and ultimately increase our chances of success for future attempts.

3. **Alignment with Purpose is Key:** What you are striving for may not always align with your true purpose. Pursuing goals that don't align with our core values can leave us feeling unfulfilled or stagnant. When we align our actions with intentionality it increases our chances for genuine satisfaction.

4. **Transform Your Perspective:** Use the questions "now what?" and "what's next?" as catalysts for motivation rather than avenues for self-pity and self-righteousness. This shift in perspective encourages proactive thinking and fosters resilience, instead of feeling entitled to success or dwelling on past setbacks.

Note: Always remember that, **how we perceive the world influences how we behave in the world.**

MOTION-BASED STAGNATION

How could we end the section of understanding the complexities of feeling stuck in life without discussing motion-based stagnation? When we discuss stagnation, we often think about "motionless" types of stagnation. However, being stuck or stagnant doesn't always means that we're not in motion. So, what qualifies your situation as stagnant if you aren't actually stuck in one place?

Let's look at a few subtopics of motion-based stagnation:

- **Direction:** Are you going in the right direction?
- **Progress:** Are you making any progress?
- **Recycled Experiences:** Are you running in circles?
- **Ineffective Repetition:** Are you running in place?

Progress & Direction: The Importance of Going the Right Way

It's easy to feel accomplished as we check off tasks and move forward in our journeys. However, if we're not heading in the right direction, those efforts may ultimately be in vain. Imagine planning a road trip to Mexico, a destination that's 16 hours away. You prepare diligently and hit the road.

Feeling accomplished after 8 hours of driving, but then realize that you've been heading north instead of south. Instead of making progress, you find yourself 24 hours away from your goal, instead of 8. This dilemma will most likely cause you to feel defeated and unmotivated to continue on, because you've been going in the wrong direction for half of your journey.

Note: This scenario illustrates a vital lesson: progress without direction is counterproductive. Wasting time, energy, and resources can lead to feelings of hopelessness and a lack of motivation. To achieve meaningful progress, it's essential to regularly assess if you are on the right path.

Recycle Experiences: Breaking the Cycle.

Sometimes, our journeys feel like a repetitive cycle, trapping us in familiar but unproductive patterns. We face the same challenges repeatedly, feeling stuck and unable to break free. This often occurs when we cling to comfort zones, traditions, and methods that no longer serves us.

Imagine a person who continually seeks romantic relationships but ends up feeling unfulfilled each time. They try the same methods—dating apps, meeting friends of friends, or going to popular bars—hoping for a different outcome. At first, there's excitement and anticipation: meeting someone new, and experiencing a fleeting sense of progress. But as time goes on, they find themselves back in familiar and unsatisfying patterns.

Note: This experience can be disheartening. By this point, you may feel like you're on a race track, going around in circles. Sure, you're moving forward but somehow ending up exactly where you started. This will cause you to feel stuck, repeating the same mistakes without exercising self-awareness or control.

Take a moment to self-reflect:

- Are there patterns or behaviors that keep bringing you back to the same place?
- What went wrong in your previous relationships?
- What lessons can you learn from your past decisions?
- What have you ignored or overlooked that's currently keeping you stuck in unhealthy cycles?

By consciously breaking these cycles and exploring new approaches, you can foster genuine growth.

Ineffective Repetition: No way forward.

Have you ever encounter a problem that seem unsolvable? A problem that gives you a sense of hopelessness? Almost like you keep running into a brick wall every time you try to move forward? This type of stagnancy occurs when the actions you take is ineffective.

Ineffective repetition occurs when we chase after what looks good on paper, rather than what truly resonates with us. Or when we make choices based on societal expectations rather than personal alignment. For instance, you might pursue a career because it looks good to others, not because it resonates with your passions or aspirations. This creates the illusion of movement: like being on a treadmill, where you're exerting effort but not actually going anywhere.

Note: The objective is to make **meaningful** and **intentional** movements that aligns with your goals and aspirations.

Part 3A: The Center of it All
Digging Deeper: Uncovering the Roots of Stagnation

Everything we go through in life is a domino effect of our own decisions, and the decisions of others. With that being said, let's dig a bit deeper to uncover **who** or **what** is the root cause of *your* stagnant seasons.

Here are 6 **categories** of self-reflecting questions that can cause us to:

1. Gain some insight to uncover root causes of our stagnation.
2. Provide guide towards making positive changes, and defying stagnation.

Categories of Self-Reflecting Questions

1. Self-Awareness & Self-Assessment
2. Personal & Professional Goals
3. Habits & Routines
4. External Influences
5. Obstacles & Barriers
6. Learning & Growing

Self-Reflecting Questions

Self-Awareness & Self-Assessment

- Do I have any unresolved emotional issues?
- Am I managing stress and anxiety well?
- Am I handling failures and setbacks well?
- How do I typically respond to challenges and obstacles?
- How effective are my decision-making skills?
- Do I have mental clarity? If not, what can I do to gain mental clarity?

Personal & Professional Goals

- What's hindering me from stepping out of my comfort zone?
- Have my short-term or long-term goals change over time? If so, why?
- Am I still passionate about the goals that I have set for myself?
- Am I managing and balancing my personal and professional life well?
- Is my career path fulfilling?
- What steps can I take to improve my work experiences?
- Am I staying up to date with changes in my career or personal interests?
- Do I have a clear understanding of what my goals and aspirations are?

Habits & Routines

- What daily habits are <u>contributing</u> to my growth?
- What daily habits are <u>hindering</u> my growth?
- Am I being consistent with the plans and routines that I've set for myself?
- Do I make enough time for self-care and rest?
- Are there areas in my life that I have neglected? If so, what are some changes that needs to be made?
- What patterns or habits am I clinging to that contributes to my stagnancy?

External Influences

- Who are the key people in my life, and how do they influence my choices?
- Are there any relationships that might be holding me back from my goals?
- Do I feel supported by my social circle?
- Are there external factors influencing my lack of progress? If so, how can I address or lessen their impact?
- Am I receiving feedback or support from <u>trusted</u> individuals to gain perspective on my situation?

Obstacles & Barriers

- What are the biggest barriers to my progress?
- Are there any recurring patterns in the obstacles that I face?
- What can I do differently to overcome my challenges?
- Am I allowing fear to hold me back from taking necessary risks?

Learning & Growing

- Am I continuously learning and seeking new experiences?
- What is the last <u>new</u> set of skills that I've learned?
- What is the last <u>new</u> experience that I've had?
- What small steps can I take today to break free from the cycle of stagnation, and move towards a more fulfilling and purposeful life?

Why are you stuck?

Once you have answered the previous self-reflecting questions, you'll be a few steps closer to defeating or avoiding stagnant seasons. Remember, the self-reflecting questions were created to answer **who** or **what** is causing your stagnation. This next section however is to answer **how** or **why** you may be experiencing stagnation.

Here are some unconventional reasons for stagnation:

⇒ Option Overload

⇒ The pervasive nature of technology

⇒ Expressing gratitude incorrectly

⇒ Unmet expectations & Misguided Motivation

Option Overload

"Limited options and resources" is a common topic to talk about when discussing stagnation. But how many of us have experienced stagnation due to having "too many options"? Although having options can be empowering, having **too many** options can be **overwhelming** and detrimental to our decision-making and productivity.

A few negative outcomes of option overload are:

◊ Decision Paralysis

◊ Analysis Paralysis

◊ Dissatisfaction

Decision Paralysis: When faced with option overload, we may struggle to take meaningful and decisive actions. The overwhelming amount of information to consider can cause us to be reluctant to commit to any particular choice.
Causing stress and anxiety.

Analysis Paralysis: Option overload can cause us to overthink and over-consider too many options. Which makes it difficult to effectively prioritize tasks and goals.
Causing distractions and scattered thoughts.

Dissatisfaction: When faced with option overload, we may second-guess our decisions, and constantly wonder if we've made the right choice. This train of thought can grow with the constant "what ifs", and "should haves".
Causing regret and unhappiness with our choices.

Note: Having a "limited" number of options can offer clarity, simplicity, and ease of decision-making. Sometimes, when our options are more confined or reduced, we may feel more **confident** with our decisions. Causing us to experience greater satisfaction with our choices.

The Pervasive Nature of Technology

"Dear Dr. Baker, what can I do to keep the overwhelming nature of technology from causing me to feel stagnant in my personal life?"

-Kerry-Ann Mores

To answer the above question, there are two strategies in mind: **Boundary Setting** and **Mindful Consumption**.

Boundary Setting: Whenever we discuss the topic of setting boundaries it's usually around the premise of human interaction. However, setting boundaries can be exercised when dealing with technology, food, and so much more. In this context, setting clear boundaries can help to create a healthy relationship with technology.

With the constant notifications, endless scrolling, and endless entertainment options, technology can easily divert our attention away from important tasks and goals. which causes a decrease in productivity. Breaking free from the overwhelming nature of technology can be accomplished by:

- Setting specific times for using technology devices.
- Setting specific times for disconnecting from it all.
- Designating *tech-free* zones in your home.
- Prioritizing face-to-face interactions.

Note: Allow yourself to fully engage in activities without the distractions of technology. Savor the moments without feeling the pressure to constantly be connected or "plugged in". By setting these boundaries, we can protect our mental well-being, and reduce feelings of being overwhelmed.

Mindful Consumption: Practice intentionality and awareness of how, when, and why we use technology. Also practice intentionality to follow accounts and platforms that **inspires, educates, uplifts,** and **promotes** personal and professional growth. These intentional actions will allow us to spend our time on contents that adds value to our lives as opposed to mindlessly scrolling and procrastinating.

When practicing mindful consumption remember that:

1. **We are what we consume:** Whether physically, intellectually, spiritually, or emotionally. So, why not focus on consuming content that nourishes us with positivity, motivation, and skills that aligns with our values?

2. **Technology should serve us, not dictate our lives:** Use technology as a tool to **enhance** our experiences, not to **control** it.

3. **Limit exposure to negativity:** Avoid content that triggers **negative emotions**, promotes **self-comparison**, and **unproductive behavior**.

4. **Be intentional with your time:** Prioritize content and activities that contribute to your growth, well-being, and goals.

Note: Setting boundaries and practicing mindful consumption to avoid feeling overwhelmed by technology is a key way to also avoid habits that causes stagnant moments. Such habits are procrastination, obsession, and isolation.

Expressing Gratitude Appropriately

An important topic that isn't discussed enough is **Gratitude Guilt**. Gratitude guilt is when we feel <u>obligated</u> to constantly express gratitude to someone in order to avoid *appearing* "ungrateful". This type of pressure can lead to <u>stagnant</u> and inauthentic relationships.

<u>Note:</u> Gratitude should come from the heart, it shouldn't be used as a tool to *prove* your gratefulness.

Ways to avoid remaining in stagnant relationships:

- Prioritize your own well-being, even if it means potentially disappointing others.

- Free yourself from any guilt or pressure that causes you to seek approval from others.

- Remember: just because someone supported you in the past, doesn't mean that you need to mold yourself into the person **they** desire you to be.

- Establish strong boundaries, and communicate them with <u>clarity</u> and <u>confidence</u>.

<u>Note:</u> When you aren't fully healed from past traumas, you may find it difficult to be assertive or uphold your boundaries. This can stem from a fear of rejection, shame, and guilt: associated with prioritizing your needs, or expressing your thoughts.

Let's Practice

> I am appreciative and grateful for the help. However, I cannot continue to feel indefinitely indebted to you. ***Gratitude is a <u>personal</u> experience that should not be demanded or expected indefinitely from anyone.***

<u>Note:</u> You aren't indebted to anyone for the rest of your life just because they helped you out of hard situations. If they feel that way, then their help wasn't and isn't genuine to begin with.

Don't allow gratitude guilt to:

- Keep you from moving on to other chapters of your life.
- Cause you to feel guilty for moving on.
- Keep you in a victim mentality.
- Keep you stagnant or stuck in a time capsule of when you needed help.
- Make you feel guilty for progressing and moving on.

<u>Note:</u> 1. Never allow your consciousness to be reduce to anyone's opinion of you and your life. **You are <u>allowed</u> to become the hero of your own story now.**

2. If your guilt is **<u>self</u>-imposed**, and not coming from the other person, work on setting clear boundaries with yourself. *Please refer to "**Navigating Stagnation: Strategic Journaling**" to help you with setting and maintaining healthy self-boundaries.*

Unmet Expectations & Misguided Motivation

Handling unmet expectations can be challenging, but it's important to remember that disappointments are a part of life, and that experiencing unmet expectations doesn't mean that you're not making progress. With that being said, let's try to not allow the disappointment of unmet expectations to cause us to **mislabel** our experiences as stagnation.

Although unmet expectation can cause us to feel stagnant, it's important to recognize that they're not the same. The emotions caused by unmet expectations is a temporary setback, while stagnation implies a complete lack of progress. When experiencing temporary setbacks, it's healthy to acknowledge the emotions that comes with it—such as anger, sadness, disappointment, and stress.

Acknowledging our negative emotions allows us to learn and grow from the experience of temporary setbacks. It also gives us the space to exercise self-reflection, rather than sitting around feeling stuck or stagnant.

Consider the following self-reflection questions:

- Are you being intentional and doing all that you can to achieve your goals and expectations?
- Are there factors beyond your control that contributed to your expectations not being met?
- Are your expectations realistic and attainable?

Note: Sometimes, adjusting our expectations can help us to find contentment in difficult situations.

Let's dig a bit deeper:

- Is this unmet expectation trying to teach you something?
- Is this unmet expectation trying to steer you into a more positive direction?
- Is this unmet expectation trying to give you a longer opportunity to perfect your craft?
- Are you mistaken this season of self-reflection and realization as a season of stagnancy?

Misguided Motivation

<u>Misguided motivation:</u> The use of dishonorable, selfish, or immoral desires to drive oneself or others toward a particular goal or action. It can involve coercion, manipulation, deceit, or other negative tactics, that compromise integrity and harm others in the process.

- *Meraki Journey Therapy*

Here are a few examples of **<u>misguided</u>** motivation:

- Comparing yourself to others.
- Striving to outshine someone else.
- Wanting to fit in with everyone else.
- Seeking attention, recognition or approval from others.
- Feeling that your progress is slower than others'.
- Desiring what someone else has.
- Lacking love for or from others.
- Feeling invisible or unworthy.
- Yearning for instant gratification and rewards.

Note: Being fixated on the fastest routes to accomplish things can result in **inner conflict**, **negative outcomes**, **loss of direction**, and **diminished core values and determination**.

Your motivation for progress should be fueled by positive intentions and desires. Here are a few **positive guided motivation**:

- Engaging in a passion or interest because it brings <u>genuine</u> joy and fulfillment.

- Setting goals that promote personal development and growth, such as:
    - Learning new skills.
    - Enhancing your mental and physical health.

- Aiming to make a <u>positive</u> impact on others, driven by empathy and compassion.

- Striving for success fueled by an <u>authentic</u> desire to reach your full potential.

- Finding purpose and meaning in actions that contribute to <u>long-term happiness</u> and fulfillment.

PRACTICAL STRATEGIES

Two practical strategies for overcoming stagnation are discipline and goal-setting.

Discipline

Sometime you're not stuck, you just lack discipline.

Discipline is the backbone of self-improvement because it ensures the sustainability of our efforts and growth. In other words, discipline provides the **structure** and **consistency** needed to maintain progress. Discipline also counteract stagnation, by establishing routines, setting clear goals, and exercising accountability.

Let's discover how discipline can help you to combat **four** key habits that contributes to stagnation:

1. Self-Doubt: Discipline encourages us to focus on positive and constructive self-talk, steering our mindset away from negativity and towards growth.

2. Compulsive Behaviors: Through discipline, we can address compulsive behaviors by practicing mindfulness techniques and replacing unhealthy habits with healthier alternatives.

3. Eating Challenges: Discipline—in this instance can compel us to meal prep, practice mindful eating, and seek professional support when necessary.

4. Procrastination: Discipline enables us to break down goals into manageable steps and commit to meeting deadlines, fostering steady progress toward our objectives.

Setting Goals

Most of us can agree that our goals should provide direction and purpose. But how many of us can agree that our goals are meant to be personal and unique to <u>who we are</u>? When our goals align with our authentic selves, we experience fulfillment and growth. However, when our goals aren't aligned with our authentic selves, we will most likely experience emptiness and stagnancy.

Needless to say, our goals shouldn't require validations from others. Seeking validation from others can lead to pursuing goals that doesn't resonate with who we truly are. Which will inevitably cause us to prioritize pleasing others, conforming to societal expectations, and risk becoming trapped in a reality that isn't meant for us.

To understand how to set authentic goals that aligns with who you truly are, follow the Meraki Journey Guideline: **E.M.P.A.T.H.**

- <u>E</u>liminate Chaos and Confusion
- <u>M</u>otivation Enhancer
- <u>P</u>rioritize Tasks
- <u>A</u>lign With Core Values
- <u>T</u>imeline Setting
- <u>H</u>armony

E.M.P.A.T.H.

Eliminate Chaos and Confusion

Organize your goals into themes or categories. Such as: academic goals, professional goals, short-term goals, family goals, etc. This approach allows us to compartmentalize our goals, and reduce chaos and confusion.

Motivation Enhancer

When setting goals, be sure to include a note after each one that explains:

- The reasons behind the goal.
- The positive impact it will have.
- Why it holds personal significance for you.

This approach will strengthen your internal motivation, and decrease the likelihood of burnout, procrastination, or self-doubt.

Prioritize Tasks

Within each category, rank your goals according to their urgency, significance, and availability of resources. This step will help you manage your time effectively, ensuring that your efforts are focused on the most critical goals first.

E.M.P.A.T.H.

Align With Core Values

Now, take a moment to review your goals. Do they align with your core values? If so, continue to the next step. And if not, revise your goals to align with *your* values, beliefs, and passions.

Timeline Setting

After ensuring that your goals aligns with your core values, let's set timelines for achieving them. These timelines should be flexible enough to adjust when necessary, yet firm enough to initiate discipline and determination.

Note: This step also allows us to track our progress effectively, and make necessary adjustments as needed.

Harmony

Make sure that your goals are balance, cohesive, and aren't conflicting. They should all contribute to a unified purpose: improving yourself and enhancing your life's experiences. When your goals are in harmony, it maximizes your overall effectiveness and fulfillment.

Part 3B: Emotions and Perceptions

Sometimes, we set goals based on fleeting emotions or temporary influences. While these choices may feel justified in the moment, they often result in outcomes that don't align with our true selves. This disconnect can leave us feeling stuck, unable to move forward.

Note: Our emotions and perceptions shape our decisions, which ultimately impact our overall lives.

For example:

1. Fear has the power to paralyze us, preventing us from taking the crucial steps needed to pursue our dreams.
2. Our biased perceptions can limit us, shutting us off from new opportunities for growth and self-improvement.

When we allow feelings to overshadow reality, it becomes easy to fall into a state of stagnation, where progress halts, and potential goes unfulfilled. Recognizing this pattern is key to realigning with our true selves, and moving forward with clarity and purpose.

Prioritizing Fear Over Reality: A Recipe for Stagnancy

We experience fear when we are *convinced* that there's a threat, risk, pain, or negative outcome lurking on the other side of a situation. When fear takes the lead, it distorts our perception of what's possible, and make it seem impossible. In other words, some **risks** may appear to be greater than they really are. Which leads to inaction that keeps us trapped in a cycle of stagnation.

Four aspects of fear that influences stagnancy:

1. **Fear of Self**
2. **Taught Fear**
3. **Fear of Change**
4. **Fear of Failure**

Fear of Self: Stuck in Surface Living

Confronting personal flaws, past mistakes, and hidden desires can be profoundly uncomfortable—which often result in the avoidance of deep self-exploration. This avoidance to look inward can block <u>self-awareness,</u> leaving us <u>stuck,</u> and unwilling to embrace the changes that could transform our lives. When we fear ourselves, we choose to live at the surface level, avoiding the deeper aspects of who we are.

This fear keeps us from exploring our true potential. It also keeps us from embracing the parts of ourselves that might feel uncomfortable or unfamiliar. By staying at this <u>shallow</u> depth, we limit our growth, settling for a life that feels safe but unfulfilling. This avoidance not only stifles personal growth but also creates a cycle of self-sabotage.

<u>We become more focused on managing appearances rather than addressing the root causes of our fears, insecurities, or unmet expectation.</u> The longer we linger at this surface level, the more we distance ourselves from meaningful transformation, and the fulfillment that comes from living authentically.

On the other hand, when we face our true selves—the good, the bad, and the unknown—we unlock the power to live deeply and intentionally. Only then can we break free from stagnation, and rise above limitations imposed by fear. It is in this deeper understanding of ourselves that we discover the courage to pursue goals that are aligned with our true nature, rather than those dictated by fleeting emotions or external expectations.

Living on the surface can manifest in various ways. Here are a few:

- **Lack of Purpose:** Living without a clear sense of purpose or direction.

- **Surface-Level Goals:** Setting goals based on societal expectations and not your own.

- **Superficial Relationships:** Focusing on social connections that lack meaning and depth.

- **Reactive Living:** Responding to life's issues without taking proactive steps for solutions.

- **Resistance to Change:** Sticking to routines or habits without questioning them.

Taught Fear: Stuck in Tradition

Taught fear can create internal barriers that prevent us from pursuing our own path, and limits our full potential.

Here are a few taught fear phrases:

1. Better safe than sorry: From a young age, this phrase has instilled in us a fear of taking opportunities that involve any level of risk. This learned fear can stifle our growth, creativity, and sense of adventure.

2. Don't rock the boat: This phrase has discouraged us from challenging the status quo—making us afraid to speaking up or fighting for what we believe is right.

3. Curiosity kills the cat: This phrase has discouraged us from exploring and questioning things. Which often instills a fear of seeking new knowledge—causing stagnancy.

Taught fear can easily be mistaken for tradition, as it is often passed down by family, culture, or society. However, it isn't uncommon for us to instill these fears within ourselves. We do this by steering clear of anything that might remind us of past failures, rejections, traumas, broken relationships, or deals that didn't work out.

This fear of reliving negative emotions teaches us that it's acceptable to stop trying after a failed attempt. Over time, it can prevent us from seizing new opportunities, experiencing love, or finding happiness. By surrendering to this fear, we allow our past to dictate our future, limiting our potential for growth and fulfillment.

To break free, we must confront this fear, understanding that failure is not a permanent state, but a stepping stone toward success. Embracing discomfort and uncertainty allows us to discover the deeper joys that come from persistence and courage.

Note: Let's use our past mistakes as motivation to explore <u>alternative approaches or solutions</u>, instead of *solely* focusing on the mistake itself. **Utilize the lessons and skills gained from your past experiences.**

Fear of Change: Stuck in a Comfort Zone

Fear of change can keep us stuck in routines, relationships, and environments that no longer serve our well-being. I understand that change can feel overwhelming, challenge our sense of security, and trigger feelings of vulnerability, anxiety, and a lack of control—even when our current situation isn't ideal. However, it's important to remember that not all uncomfortable feelings are signs of something negative.

Imagine wearing a cast after breaking an arm. It's uncomfortable, itchy, and might even make you feel claustrophobic. But does that mean that the cast is harming you? Of course not. In fact, the cast is essential for healing and repairing. In the same way, change—though uncomfortable—can help repair what's broken in your life if done with intentionality.

Note: Remember that discomfort is often a sign of growth, not harm.

Moving Forward:

1. **Cultivate Curiosity and Adaptability:** Approach change with a mindset of curiosity—eager to explore new possibilities.

2. **View Change as an Opportunity:** Instead of seeing change as a threat, recognize it as a chance for growth.

3. **Focus on What You <u>Can</u> Control:** You may not be in control of the change itself, but you can control how you respond to uncertainty.

4. **Learn from Setbacks:** Each setback is a lesson, building your confidence in navigating future challenges.

Fear of Failure: Stuck in Self-Doubt

    The fear of failure can feel so overwhelming that we often convince ourselves that it's safer to not try at all. However, if we allow fear to become stronger than our will to thrive, we will risk limiting our potential, and hindering meaningful successes. Instead, let's try to find ways to challenge ourselves by pursuing new opportunities that are necessary for personal growth—thus, overcoming phases of stagnancy.

<u>Overcoming the Fear of Failure:</u>

1. Embrace Failure as a Teacher: Recognize that failure is a natural part of the learning process, offering opportunities to grow and adapt.

2. Shift Your Perspective: Perceive failure as valuable feedback, and a chance to improve, rather than a reflection of your self-worth.

3. Set Realistic Goals: Break down your goals into manageable steps, making them easier to tackle. Which <u>can</u> lower the chances of failing.

4. Take <u>Calculated</u> Risks: Gradually expose yourself to taking risks. This will build your confidence and bravery to "try".

5. Challenge Self-Sabotaging Thoughts: Avoid thoughts that undermine your confidence, such as:

- I'm not worthy.
- I'm not good enough.
- I'm trapped in this space.
- I'm not meant for that.
- I can't go on anymore.

Break Free from Self-Sabotage
Overthinking Prison

Fear can be a powerful force that keeps us stuck in a cycle of overthinking. Therefore, if you find yourself feeling stagnant, it's important take a moment to examine the patterns of your thoughts. To help with this process, let's explore four common types of overthinking that can keep us stagnant: **S. H. O. W.**

1. Social Anxiety
2. Hyperanalyzing the Past
3. Overanalyzing Decisions and Situations
4. Worrying About the Future

Dr. Christina Baker

<u>S</u>. <u>H</u>. O. W.

1. Social anxiety

Social anxiety stems from an overwhelming fear of judgment or rejection in social situations. This fear often leads to **avoidance behaviors**: Steering clear of social interactions or activities that could help us grow. By isolating ourselves, we tend to miss out on valuable experiences, relationships, and opportunities that are essential for personal development and progression.

Note: To break free from social anxiety, challenge yourself to engage with others, even when it feels uncomfortable. <u>Every new connection could be a beautiful step towards growth and success.</u>

2. Hyperanalyzing the Past

Dwelling on the past is like being stuck in a mental loop, constantly replaying old scenarios, and dwelling on what could have or should have been. While reflecting on past experiences can be valuable, <u>fixation</u> is not. This kind of overthinking robs us of the ability to move forward, take new steps toward our goals, and to seize new opportunities.

Note: Remember, we can't move forward if all our attention is stuck on where we've been.

S. H. <u>O</u>. <u>W</u>.

3. Overanalyzing Decisions & Situations

Overanalyzing traps us in a cycle of indecision. We become so preoccupied with every possible outcome that we're unable to make any choice at all. It's like wandering aimlessly in a maze, where the more we search for the perfect exit, the more lost we become. Overthinking is like quicksand—the harder we try to reason our way out, the deeper we sink. To break free, we must release the need for certainty, and trust ourselves to take decisive action.

Note: Trust your instincts, and take decisive steps toward your goals, even if the path isn't perfectly clear.

4. Worrying About the Future

Similar to being fixated on the past, constant worrying about the future can also contribute to stagnation. When our minds are preoccupied with potential future failures or obstacles, we lose sight of the opportunities that exist in the <u>present</u>.

How can we navigate the road in front of us, if we're intensely focused on the distant horizon?

Breaking Free From the Cycle of Overthinking
Acknowledgment and Accountability

Fear is a natural emotional response, triggered by our past experiences, and reinforced by social conditioning. These influences shape how we perceive the world, but they can also distort our thoughts, behaviors, and decision-making. The more we allow fear to dominate our thinking, the more control it exerts over our lives. This is why it's so important to take ownership of our thoughts—whether positive or negative, they ultimately determine the <u>direction</u> of our lives, and shape the reality we experience.

- **Negative**: Self-defeating thoughts act like barriers, keeping us stuck and limiting our potential.
- **Positive**: Empowering thoughts open up possibilities, and foster a more optimistic life.

Note: Remember sometimes, the only barriers holding us back are the ones we create in our minds. Therefore:

- Stop undermining yourself with constant self-doubt. *You are more capable than you realize.*
- Silence the inner critic that thrives on negative self-talk.
- Break free from the cycle of overthinking, which often leaves you feeling stuck and paralyzed.

When you confront the fears that fuel your overthinking, you reclaim your mental space. This shift allows you to move beyond stagnation, restoring a sense of clarity and purpose to your life. *Remember: clarity leads to action, and action leads to growth.*

> Let go of the burdens of the past, and the anxieties of the future. Instead, channel your energy on actions you can take <u>today</u> to shape the tomorrow you desire.

Breaking Free From the Cycle of Pain

At times, overthinking can serve as the very barrier that keeps us trapped and stagnant in life. Overcoming mental barriers offers the significant benefit of freeing yourself from past traumas. When we hold on to unresolved traumas, they can create mental barriers that prevents us from moving forward, and fully engaging with life.

These barriers may show up as fear, self-doubt, or an endless loop of past events—*keeping you stuck in a cycle of pain*. By seeing the link between your past and the obstacles you face today, you'll understand that overcoming mental barriers isn't just about changing your present thoughts—it's also about healing the past wounds that have created your mental barriers in the first place.

We can start this process by:

- Reflecting on how our past traumas have shaped our current mindset and behaviors.

- Understanding that the mental barriers we face today may stem from unresolved emotional wounds from the past.

- Taking steps to address past traumas through therapy, self-reflection, or other healing practices.

- Creating a new reality that is not defined by past pain, but by our capacity for growth and healing.

- Freeing ourselves from the limitations imposed by past traumas.

The way we interpret events and the meanings we attach to them can either trigger emotional wounds or intensify their impact on our mental well-being. This is why prioritizing mental health is crucial—it forms the foundation of how we experience life. When we remain stuck in our pain, it feeds into mistrust, paranoia, depression, anxiety, isolation, and countless other emotional burdens.

These mental and emotional challenges make it difficult to make decisions that lead to happiness. They also block us from forming meaningful relationships, whether they are platonic, romantic, professional, or familial.

In short, untreated emotional pain prevents us from living a full, connected life. By nurturing our mental health, we allow healing to take place. This opens the door to greater emotional well-being, personal growth, and meaningful relationships.

Note: Taking care of your mental health doesn't just benefit you—it strengthens the connections you build with others.

By nurturing our mental health, we:
- Deepen our connections with others.
- Empower ourselves to break free from the patterns that hold us back.
- Gain resilience and clarity.
- Gain a stronger sense of self and purpose.
- Redefine our narratives and create a life that aligns with our true desires.

Stuck in Trauma

Our gifts can only take us as far as our healing.

Over the years we've been hearing the same solutions to trauma—just wrapped in different words. But what if—beyond self-forgiveness and the avoidance of trauma triggers—we chose not to 'heal'? Well, in the traditional sense at least. What if, instead of trying to return to who we were *before* the trauma, we transform trauma into a source of power?

But before digging any deeper into this unconventional solution, let's first discuss a few basics.

Trauma is such a complex topic that has been studied and discussed for decades. Yet still there's a crucial aspect of it that's often left unaddressed.

Trauma isn't just about what has <u>happened</u> to us in the past; it's also about how we <u>respond</u> to those experiences. In other words, the way we perceive and react to our past can intensify the impact of trauma in our lives.

For example:

- Judging ourselves for the choices we've made.
- Blaming ourselves for how others have treated us.
- Replaying painful memories and reliving the emotions attached to them.
- Believing that we are unworthy or undeserving of healing and happiness.

These reactions are known as <u>Trauma Responses</u>.

Understanding Trauma Responses

A trauma response refers to the way an individual reacts to stressful situations that overwhelm their ability to cope. These responses vary from person to person and can manifest in a variety of ways. Such as: psychologically, emotionally, or physically. A few common symptoms include self-blaming, anxiety, fear, depression, hypervigilance, inaction, or avoidance behaviors.

Any form of harmful behavior toward another person is undoubtedly wrong. However, how we choose to respond to those behaviors can either help us heal or trap us in a cycle of pain. It's often said, "Our emotions are valid, but our behavior is not." This suggests that while the emotions we feel when wronged are justified, how we respond to those emotions can put us in the wrong.

At **Meraki Journey Therapy**, we believe this statement only tells part of the story. Emotions are not just a reaction—they are shaped by our mental capacity and the way we've learned to process the world around us. This means that no matter someone's age, they may lack the mental tools to truly grasp and process certain emotions. Yes, emotions are natural and valid, but what causes one person to feel deeply hurt by something that might not affect someone else at all?

Note: Emotions are often driven by our perspective and the thought patterns we've developed.

Trauma distorts our thinking, often leading to cognitive patterns like catastrophizing. This term means to always expect the worst, or to see situations as more dire than they truly are. Catastrophizing has the power to fuel negative emotions and cloud our perception of reality. At **Meraki Journey**, we teach techniques to recognize and dismantle these harmful thought patterns. By doing so, we can replace them with healthier, more balanced perspectives.

Note: Elevating our thought patterns isn't just about changing how we think—it's about <u>transforming how we live</u>. It's a journey toward honoring both our past and our potential. But how do we elevate our thought patterns to rise above the pain and confusion that trauma brings?

The key to elevating our thought patterns lies in cultivating an internal dialogue where the most mature, wise version of ourselves engages directly with our place of brokenness. Imagine this version of you as a compassionate guide—someone who has weathered storms and emerged with wisdom and understanding. By allowing this wiser self to speak to the vulnerable parts of you, you create a powerful, ongoing conversation that transforms your inner landscape.

This internal dialogue is not stagnant; it's a living, breathing exchange that evolves as you do. As your wiser self listens to, and acknowledges your pain, fears, and doubts, it gently challenges the distorted thoughts that have taken root. It offers new perspectives, reframing your experiences in a way that promotes healing and growth. Over time, this dialogue helps you to see beyond the immediate pain and confusion, allowing you to rise above the limitations imposed by trauma.

Your thought patterns begin to shift, naturally aligning with a more balanced, hopeful, and empowered way of thinking. This process is not about denying your struggles, but rather about honoring them with a response that reflects your highest self—a response that transforms <u>hurt into healing</u>, and <u>confusion into clarity</u>.

Here's how to elevate your thought patterns:

- **Focus on <u>solutions</u> more than problems:** Shift your attention to what can be done.
- **Practice self-compassion:** Treat yourself with the same kindness and understanding that you would offer to a cherished friend.
- **Surrounding yourself with intelligent and inspiring people:** Their influence can spark new ideas and perspectives that elevates your thinking.
- **Challenge irrational beliefs:** Question thoughts that don't serve you, and replace them with those rooted in truth and possibilities.
- **Engage in activities that increases positivity and growth:** Whether it's through hobbies, learning, or physical activities, these actions help to reinforce elevated thinking.
- **Foster flexibility in how you perceive and respond to situations:** Adaptability is key to maintaining a balanced mindset, even in the face of adversity.

Note: The following steps can help us engage with our emotions in a healthier, more constructive way. While the same emotions may surface, how we respond to them will change. This shift in both action and perspective is a great way to lessen the hold that past trauma has over us.

The past trauma that has a strong grip on me...

When I was a child a punishment that I had was, my mother stripped me naked, and I had to stand in the middle of our home, with my siblings and family members walking past me for hours. I felt sad and ashamed, but as a child, I couldn't fully grasp the impact of what was happening or how it would shape me as an adult. Now, as I've grown older, I'm beginning to understand just how deeply that trauma embedded itself into my psyche. Back then, my young mind wasn't mature enough to identify or process what I was feeling, but that doesn't mean the trauma wasn't real or deeply damaging.

Lacking the mental capacity or emotional maturity to handle those feelings, I spent many years acting out in ways that weren't aligned with my growth in other areas of my life. It took time for me to truly understand what I had gone through; and to realize that the current me needed to take care of the broken parts of my younger self. I needed to give my inner child the attention and <u>tools</u> to respond in a wiser more mature way.

-Anonymous sharer

How we respond to stress, negative behaviors, and challenging experiences can be the very response that truly traumatizes us. Our thought processes significantly influence how we perceive and internalize traumatic experiences. When we are fixated on the past—constantly questioning why things happened the way that they did, or what could have or should have been done differently—we risk deepening our feelings of regret, betrayal, abandonment, shame, and guilt.

Many people have faced abuse or hardship, yet not everyone emerges in the same way. Some may use humor as a coping mechanism, while others might be deeply scarred by their experiences. Have you ever listened to someone's story and think, "I wouldn't have survived that", or "I would have been severely traumatized by that".

- → So, what are we missing here?
- → Is it the event itself, or is it how we perceive that event that actually causes trauma?
- → Why do some people seem to move on with their lives, while others remain trapped in their pain?

Trauma has a way of pulling us into an endless loop of unresolved questions and imagined scenarios. We might find ourselves replaying events, thinking of what could have or should have happened if only we had been braver, stronger, or if life had unfolded differently. But these imagined versions of reality are not the truth—they are mental traps that keep us anchored to the past, preventing us from healing and growing in the present.

Yes, it's true that we were wronged—sometimes by the very people who were meant to protect us. But by feeding the pain with negative thoughts and trauma-driven responses, we add to our own suffering. Holding on to past hurts only deepens our distress, creating barriers that block the path to healing, and keeping us stuck where we no longer need to be.

Shift Your Perspective: Instead of dwelling on what we cannot change, let's focus on what we can—our perceptions and our reactions. In this moment and moving forward, we have the power to choose a different path. We can become more disciplined, braver, stronger, and wiser than we were before. By shifting our focus to the present and the future, we reclaim our strength and open the doors to true healing.

The Link Between Trauma and Stagnation
Reconstruct Your Path

When our trauma responses become ingrained in our daily habits and ways of thinking, we find ourselves stagnant and unable to move forward. This type of stagnation isn't just a pause; it's a sign that we're still tied to the pain of our past. To break free from this cycle, we must first understand how deeply intertwined **trauma** and **stagnation** are in our lives.

Instead of striving for perfection or an idealized version of healing, let's focus on building resilience: the capacity to recover from setbacks and adapt to change, rather than avoiding discomfort and inconvenience. Let's also learn to embrace the ups and downs of our journey.

Here are a few steps to consider:

1. Identify Signs of Trauma-Induced Stagnation
2. Acknowledge Your Pain Without Judgment
3. Reflect on How Trauma Has Shaped Your Beliefs
4. Reframe Your Narrative

For example: Identify Signs of Trauma-Induced Stagnation

Emotional Reactions: Anxiety, anger, overwhelm, or sadness.

Physical Symptoms: Muscle tension, fatigue, difficulty sleeping, or headaches.

Behavioral Patterns: Withdrawal from others, Avoidance, impulsiveness, difficulty trusting, overreacting, or seeking distractions to escape emotional pain.

Identifying Unresolved Trauma

To connect the dots between our past and present experiences, it's crucial to observe recurring patterns in our physical and emotional reactions. Pay close attention to signs such as tension, changes in breathing, sudden mood swings, or heightened agitation in response to certain people or situations. Recognizing these patterns can reveal how unresolved past traumas continues to affect the way we response to things in the present.

To help uncover these patterns, consider answering the following questions:

1. Do you often feel anxious or overwhelmed in situations where others seem relaxed? What's triggering this type of response?
2. Are there specific people or places that make you feel scared, powerless, or like you want to *escape*? Why do you think that happens?
3. How do these feelings impact your thoughts and actions now? Do you notice any habits that hold you back?
4. When you feel emotional distress, what physical sensations do you notice? How do they affect your daily life?
5. Do you find yourself facing the same issues or conflicts repeatedly? What patterns do you see in your responses?
6. How do you usually deal with emotional discomfort? Are your coping methods helping you or making things worse?
7. In what ways do you think your past experiences are influencing your choices and relationships today?

Lord Grant Me Grace On My Journey To Healing

Unresolved trauma has significantly impacted my relationships and trust. It has made me hesitant to connect with others and skeptical of their love and care, especially since those who were supposed to protect me the most has caused wounds so deep that I am not yet ready to fully confront. This unresolved pain has led me to blame myself for my pain, feel unlovable, and withdrawn from social and professional opportunities. I know I have some more healing to do in order to get out of this mindset, but <u>how can I heal from wounds that I'm afraid of confronting?</u>

Dr. Baker, thank you for teaching me that the **journey to healing starts with acknowledging that these feelings exist and seeking to understand them.** By gently exploring and addressing my hidden wounds, I can gradually uncover their impact, and work towards rebuilding trust, enhancing connections, and embracing my worth. Thanks for giving me the tools to be patient and compassionate with myself on this journey to healing.

-Teirra Morgan

Sabotaging Your Healing
Self-sabotage is a trauma-based response that cause stagnation.

It's common to want to reach out to the person who have wronged you in order to "get some sort of closure". However, this response can inadvertently worsen your trauma, especially if your offender:

- Fails to express any remorse.
- Denies the wrongdoing.
- Has *selective* amnesia.
- Remains unchanged or unaffected.

Self-sabotage extends beyond prematurely ending a relationship due to the fear of rejection. Any behavior or habit that causes interruptions or delays in your healing journey is considered to be self-sabotage. Please don't use closure as an excuse to revisit a harmful situation or person. Closure starts with changed behavior—*your* behavior. Which includes the way you think, the way you respond, and the way you see yourself.

Trauma can cause lasting effects on us, but does this mean that we are doomed and unable to move forward? Does this mean that the rest of our lives are out of our hands? No. Let's learn how to take responsibility for our current and future actions. Let's not allow trauma to keep us stagnant. Let's not continue to blame our current behaviors on past experiences.

For example: "I'm like this because…". This too is a form of self-sabotage.

For far too long, I found myself trapped in a cycle of seeking closure and healing that felt just out of reach. I repeatedly turned to my father, yearning for validation and understanding, only to be met with dismissal that shattered my spirit even further. It was a painful realization, but I now understand that my healing journey is not contingent upon him or anyone else; it is fundamentally about me. I refuse to sit idly by, waiting for him to change or to confront his own traumas before I can begin to heal.

What happens if the very people who could offer him closure are no longer alive or simply unwilling? Does that mean I am destined to remain in this state of emotional limbo? Absolutely not. His journey of self-improvement and apologies is his to navigate, while my path to healing and transformation is entirely mine.

I owe a profound debt of gratitude to you, Dr. Baker for your invaluable counseling. You have illuminated the truth that I should never sabotage my own healing by relinquishing power to someone else. I am reclaiming my journey, embracing the fullness of my experience, and moving forward with strength and purpose.

-Grace Miller

> Healing isn't just about being free from the traumatizing thoughts of what has happened to you. <u>It's about changed behavior and changed mindset.</u> So, even though you may not feel the pain of the trauma anymore, how you respond to things can indicate whether you may be struggling with elevating past your traumas.

Journal Entry:

Dear Chrissy,

It's time to stop giving your past all the power to control your present and future. You can't control how others choose to behave or treat you, but you can control yourself. You can control your reactions to things. You can control the roster of who stays in your life and who goes. You can control which memories you choose to highlight, glorify, and give reverence to.

It's okay now. You are safe. Please stop retraumatizing yourself by revisiting things and people who should stay in the past. A beautiful and healed lifestyle has been waiting for you to choose it.

You can't force anyone to love and treat you right. Reparent yourself instead of going back to a parent who keeps abusing you and breaking your heart. Re-teach yourself instead of being stuck on what your parents should and could have done.

Re-love yourself instead of desperately seeking love to fill the gap of what wasn't given to you. Re-acknowledge yourself instead of fighting to be "unrejected". Take <u>charge</u> in giving yourself what you need instead unhealthily seeking it from others.

*Once you do the work that needs to be done, the right people will come along, and they **will** stay. Your healed behavior and mindset will keep you from sabotaging it. I'm sorry that you had to go through all the things that you went through. But you are safe now. You are free. And you are more than I could ever thank God for.*

Remember: you have zero control over anyone's healing but my own.

-Chrissy

Acknowledge Your Pain Without Judgment: Self-Forgiveness

Allow yourself to feel your emotions without judgment or criticism. Understand that your past emotional responses were once necessary for survival, even if they no longer serve you today. This act of self-compassion is the first step in moving away from a survival mode to a growth mindset. For this process to be effective, acknowledgment must be paired with acceptance. Acceptance doesn't mean surrendering to the pain, but to acknowledge its existence and impact. In other words, accept that negative emotions and painful memories are a natural part of human existence.

What better way to acknowledge your pain than forgiving yourself for being a part of the reason for the pain? Forgiveness is a powerful multi-step process to release yourself from the hold of past wounds. So, let's start with <u>self</u>-forgiveness. Understand that forgiving yourself is an act of self-love that empowers you to live more authentically and freely. Here's how:

1. Forgive yourself for not having the necessary tools you needed in those difficult time, and focus on doing better in the future.

2. Forgive yourself for the negative reactions and mistakes you've made up to this point.

3. Release yourself from the emotional burdens tied to past experiences and actions —such as guilt, shame, or self-blame.

4. Acknowledge the courage it takes to face your mistakes and honor the effort you've made in trying to improve.

5. Recognize that holding onto self-blame only prevents you from experiencing inner peace and joy.

Reflect on How Trauma Has Shaped Your Beliefs

When trauma shapes our lives, it's easy to find ourselves in a constant state of alertness—always on edge, waiting for threats, whether they're real or just in our minds. Over time, this can pull us away from our true selves, leaving us feeling disconnected. But it's important to reconnect with who we really are. This begins by taking a closer look at how those traumatic experiences have influenced the way we see ourselves and the world around us.

When you're stuck in survival mode, it's hard to grow or move forward. Breaking free from stagnation requires understanding the roots of your emotional patterns and beliefs. Only then can you begin to challenge those old narratives and create space for healing, growth, and transformation. By reconnecting with your inner self, you unlock the power to move beyond the past, and step into a future where you're no longer defined or limited by what's happened to you.

Reconnecting with yourself also means facing the beliefs you've carried for so long—beliefs that may be keeping you stuck. Trauma has a way of shaping how we view ourselves and the world, often creating stories that reinforce feelings of unworthiness, fear, or mistrust.

To begin this process of reconnection, it's helpful to ask yourself some honest questions:

- Do I believe that I'm unworthy of love, success, and happiness?
- Do I see the world as a hostile or dangerous place?
- What has caused me to believe these things?
- Are my beliefs based on facts, or are they shaped by my perception of pain?

This reflection will help you to discover what it feels like to be authentically you—beyond the pain and the protective barriers you've built over time. Your internal dialogue plays a crucial role in shaping both your trauma response and your recovery. By paying attention to the thoughts and narratives you tell yourself, you can start to shift away from limiting beliefs.

Turn away from behaviors that distort your inner dialogue, such as:

- Self-blaming or feeling unworthy of better treatment.
- Believing that change or improvement is unattainable.
- Isolating yourself due to past hurt, leading to mistrust of others.
- Convincing yourself that seeking support or expressing vulnerability equals weakness—preventing you from opening up.

Reframe Your Narrative
Crafting a life that reflects your strength and aspirations.

To embark on a meaningful healing journey, start by transforming the narrative around your trauma. Rather than defining yourself solely as a victim of your experiences, embrace the identity of a survivor—someone who has faced adversity and emerged with the capacity to heal and flourish. This shift in perspective allows you to view your past not as a series of unchangeable events, but as chapters in a story of resilience and personal growth.

Rewrite your story with an emphasis on the strength you've discovered within yourself and the lessons you've learned. Reflect on how these challenges have shaped you into a person with deeper insight, greater empathy, and a renewed sense of purpose. This approach not only acknowledges the pain you've endured, but also celebrates your journey toward empowerment and recovery.

Create Boundaries: In your healing journey, establishing boundaries is crucial for protecting your well-being. Start by identifying the people, environments, and situations that hinder your progress or reopen old wounds. Once you've recognized these influences, take proactive steps to safeguard your space and energy. This might involve limiting time spent with certain individuals, removing yourself from toxic environments, or gracefully declining invitations to events that have the potential of emotionally draining you.

Setting boundaries isn't about severing ties impulsively; it's about being intentional and mindful of how your interactions impact your healing. By doing so, you affirm your commitment to your growth and self-care. Remember, boundaries are essential declarations of your worth and your right to a peaceful life. By creating a nurturing environment that honors your needs, you lay a strong foundation for a healthier, more fulfilling journey ahead.

Note: As we untangle trauma from our habits and beliefs, let's embrace new experiences. Though uncomfortable at first, stepping out of your comfort zone is vital for healing and growth.

From now on, we are in control of our responses. So, let's learn to:

- **Recognize our emotions as they arise** without immediately acting on them. Acknowledge how you feel, but give yourself permission to pause before reacting.
- **Practice grounding techniques** such as deep breathing, mindfulness, or progressive muscle relaxation to calm your nervous system. These techniques can help you to stay present and centered during challenging moments.
- **Reflect on Triggers:** Take time to identify what triggers strong emotional reactions in you. Understanding these triggers allows you to prepare and respond more thoughtfully.

Note: The goal is to create space between feeling and reacting, allowing you time to choose responses that align with your true self rather than your trauma.

Trauma Response Questions (TRQs):

Trauma response questions often stem from the deep pain and confusion that trauma creates. They reflect the inner struggles of trying to make sense of experiences that were unfair, harmful, or neglectful. However, while these questions are natural, they can also keep us stuck in the past.

- What did I do wrong?
- Why didn't I recognize the signs of abuse earlier?
- Why didn't I cut them off as an adult, instead of allowing them to continue to hurt me?
- Why can't I let go of the pain, even after so much time has passed?
- Am I worthy of love and respect despite their treatment?
- Why didn't anyone protect me or intervene?
- Why do I struggle to forgive myself when I didn't cause the harm?
- Why do I feel responsible for fixing my offenders' issues?
- Why do I still feel guilty for setting boundaries?
- Why do I feel ashamed of what happened to me?
- Why do I still feel like I'm to blame for what happened?

These questions, while natural, reflect the lingering grip trauma can have on our beliefs and self-worth. Recognizing them allows you to begin shifting your perspective and asking more empowering questions that promote healing.

Empowering Questions

When we shift from survival mode to growth mode, we might start to ask ourselves more empowering and forward-focused questions, like:

- What can I learn from this experience to help me grow?
- How can I reclaim my power and heal from this?
- What boundaries can I set now to protect my peace and well-being?
- How can I show myself the love and respect I deserve?
- Who are the supportive people in my life that I can lean on?
- How can I focus on my own healing rather than feeling responsible for others?
- What steps can I take today to prioritize my emotional and mental health?
- How can I transform my pain into strength and resilience?
- How can I turn this experience into a stepping stone for becoming the best version of myself?
- What strengths or skills have I discovered in myself through overcoming this challenge, and how can I use them moving forward?

Note: These questions will help us to move from being stuck in the past to focusing on our healing, growth, and the future.

Bound By Your Words
The Complexities of Actions And Reactions

How often do we quickly label someone as "bipolar" or diagnose them with another personality disorder during a tense or unpleasant interaction? It's easy to let emotions take over in difficult moments, but it's important to remember that the person in front of you may be going through a challenging phase in their life. And their behavior might reflect coping mechanisms shaped by past trauma, or perhaps they've never had the opportunity to learn healthier ways of handling conflict and stress.

> **Trauma has a funny way of tattooing itself on the walls of our hearts and minds. And sometimes the ink used is invisible to those around you. In other words, the pain, fear, or confusion someone carries might manifest in behaviors that are easily misunderstood. What looks like drama or problematic behavior on the surface might actually be a silent cry for help—a reflection of wounds that have yet to be healed.**

Instead of attaching labels—whether to yourself or to others—consider focusing on understanding the root causes of these behaviors. By digging deeper into the "why" behind actions, you can gain valuable insights that lead to more effective responses. This shift in perspective not only cultivates empathy and patience; it also promotes personal growth. Which encourages us to offer support instead of judgment—both to ourselves and others.

Part 3C: Breaking Free From Mental Instability

By confronting stagnation and financial anxiety head-on, you can pave the way for positive self-transformation and mental stability.

Have you ever felt like you're running in place, stuck in a cycle that leaves you feeling mentally unstable and stifled in your growth? It's becoming increasingly clear that we're grappling with a mental health crisis. But how did we get to this point? Where did it all start? Has it been lurking under old, cultural taboos, making it difficult to discuss openly? Or maybe we've been so fixated on diagnosing extreme conditions like schizophrenia that we've overlooked the quieter struggles, such as the sense of stagnation?

Although stagnation isn't a mental illness, if left unaddressed, it can be the starting point for mental instabilities and other issues. In today's world where:

- The ever-changing pop culture trends are dominating our lives.
- So many people are comparing themselves to others on social media.
- Pandemics are popping up all over.

Understanding the impact of stagnation on our mental stability and personal growth is crucial.

Note: Mental instability refers to the chaotic mix of emotions and thoughts that lead to challenges like overwhelming feelings, self-doubt, strained relationships, and impaired problem-solving. All of which can contribute to stagnation in life.

When it comes to feeling stuck in life, there are many situations that can impact our mental health.
A few common impacts are:

- **Disconnection:** A sense of isolation from people and experiences.

- **Existential Crisis:** Questioning your purpose or direction in life.

- **Relationship Struggles:** Difficulties in maintaining healthy and fulfilling relationships.

- **Financial Stress:** Anxiety about financial stability and future security.

Let's briefly examine why financial stress is especially important to include when discussing the correlation between stagnation and mental instability.

> **Financial Stress:** Anxiety that stems from concerns about one's financial situation. The constant feeling of unease financially, or the fear of not knowing if you'll be okay financially in the future. Financial anxiety can significantly affect our overall well-being and mental health.

Tackling financial anxiety begins with financial literacy. If you're feeling overwhelmed, take intentional steps to regain control. Start by creating a budget to understand where you currently stand. Then reach out for support from financial advisors, counselors, or community resources that specialize in financial education. Remember, you don't have to walk alone on this journey.

Physical Manifestation of Mental Instability

Mental breakdowns rarely announce themselves with a loud crash. Instead, they creep in quietly, showing up in ways that can easily be overlooked. While the term "mental breakdown" might suggest a purely psychological experience, it's much more complex than that. It affects our mind, body, and emotions. The real challenge is learning to recognize the early signs before things spiral out of control.

A mental breakdown isn't a sign of failure or weakness. It's simply our body and mind signaling to us that they're overwhelmed. By becoming aware of these signals early, we give ourselves the power to step in and make adjustments before things get worse. The sooner we acknowledge what's happening, the better our chances are of steering ourselves back on course, and in control.

Though each person's experience is unique, there are common warning signs to look for.

- Feeling more anxious than usual.
- Growing irritability that's difficult to shake.
- Patience running thin.
- Sleeping and eating habits changing.

These aren't just fleeting emotions—they're the early whispers from our mind and body, urging us that something is wrong.

Intentional Alignment: A Path to Mental Stability
What are you equally and unequally yoked to?

In this book, we've explored a variety of topics, solutions, techniques, and concepts aimed at overcoming stagnation and its lingering effects. However, there's one more critical subject to address—the importance of intentional alignment. But what does this mean? How does intentional alignment reduce mental instability?

To grasp the full importance of <u>intentional alignment</u>, we must first understand the concept of being equally and unequally yoked with something or someone.

- **Balanced Partnership:** Being equally yoked is not just a metaphor but a powerful symbol of synergy. It represents a relationship or partnership where beliefs, values, and goals are in sync, creating a harmonious and mutually supportive bond.

- **Unbalanced Partnership:** Conversely, being unequally yoked signifies a misalignment—a situation where differences in core beliefs, values, or goals create tension and discord; preventing true connection and growth.

For a moment, think about a specific relationship or connection that holds importance in your life—whether it's platonic, romantic, familial, professional, or even your relationship with the environment around you. Now, imagine this relationship as a car, where one side represents <u>you</u>, and the other side represents the <u>environment,</u> or the <u>person</u> involved.

Question 1: How can the car move forward if one side is steering left while the other side is steering right?

It cannot. Without alignment, the car becomes immobilized, trapped in a state of resistance, breaking down under the strain, and ultimately suffering setbacks. The lesson here is clear: for any relationship or bond to progress, both sides must be aligned, moving together in the same direction.

Question 2: Do your goals, behaviors, and values align with those of the person or environment you're connected to?

If your answer is "no," you are likely unequally yoked. This misalignment isn't just a minor inconvenience; it's a source of inner turmoil, stress, and stagnation. When we are unequally yoked, the conflict between our inner world and our external reality prevents us from advancing with clarity and purpose.

Question 3: Is the environment you're in conducive to your well-being and success?

If your answer is "no," it's a strong indicator that you are unequally yoked. An environment that doesn't support your growth and well-being can hinder your progress, and cultivate instability in your mind and spirit. It's crucial to evaluate whether your surroundings are helping you thrive or holding you back.

Misalignment with others can cause mental instability in several profound ways:

Increased Stress: Misalignment often leads to continuous stress due to unresolved conflicts, unmet expectations, and the pressure to conform. Chronic stress is a significant contributor to mental health issues, including anxiety, depression, and burnouts.

Inner Conflict: When you are misaligned with someone—whether in values, beliefs, or goals—this creates a constant internal struggle. You may feel torn between staying true to yourself and trying to accommodate the other person's perspective. This internal conflict can lead to anxiety, stress, and a sense of being unsettled.

Identity Erosion: Misalignment often forces you to compromise or suppress your true self in order to maintain the relationship. Over time, this can leave you feeling lost, confused, or disconnected from who you really are. This loss of self can manifest as depression or a deep sense of dissatisfaction.

Lack of Support: In an aligned relationship or environment, you typically find mutual support and understanding. Misalignment, however, can result in a lack of emotional or psychological support, leaving you feeling isolated or misunderstood. This isolation can exacerbate feelings of loneliness or despair.

Note: When we're misaligned with someone, we often face ongoing conflicts or disagreements. This constant resistance drains us. Making it difficult to focus on personal growth or pursue our goals. Instead of moving forward, we're stuck dealing with the friction caused by these differences. In essence, to break free from this stagnation, it's essential to seek alignment in your relationships, environment, and within yourself.

Overcoming Stagnation Caused by Misalignment:

→ **Self-Reflection**
- **Awareness of Surrounding**
- **Continuous Reassessment**

Self-Reflection

Identify Core Values and Beliefs: Taking time to deeply understand your own values, beliefs, and goals.

- What matters most to you?
- What do you stand for?
- How do your values align with your current life choices?
- What fears or insecurities might be influencing your goals?
- Are there any areas where your actions contradict your core values?
- In what ways are you compromising your beliefs for external approval?
- What would you do differently if you were not concerned with others' opinions?

Note: Knowing the answers to these questions will deepen your introspection, and help you to recognize when and where misalignment occurs, and how it contribute to your stagnation.

> **Overcoming Stagnation Caused by Misalignment:**

- **Self-Reflection**
→ **Awareness of Surrounding**
- **Continuous Reassessment**

Awareness of Surrounding

Assess Your Current Relationships and Environments:
Reflecting on the people and situations in your life.

- Are they supportive of your values and goals?
- Do they contribute to your growth or hold you back?
- How do they respond to your successes and failures?
- Do they encourage or discourage your growth and ambitions?
- How have these relationships evolve over time?
- How do you feel after spending time with them—energized or depleted?
- Do they align with the person you are becoming—not just the person you were?

Note: If realignment isn't possible or the relationship is causing more harm than good, consider distancing yourself. <u>Surround yourself with people and environments that support your growth.</u>

Overcoming Stagnation Caused by Misalignment:

- **Self-Reflection**
- **Awareness of Surrounding**
- → **Continuous Reassessment**

Continuous Reassessment

Regularly Reevaluate Your Alignment: Life is dynamic, and alignment is not a one-time achievement but an ongoing process.

- Regularly assess your relationships, environments, and goals to ensure they remain in harmony with who you are, and who you want to become.
- Examine if your daily habits and routines support your goals and aspirations.
- Reevaluate your boundaries to make sure that they still serve and protect your well-being.
- Consider whether your goals are still relevant or need to be adjusted based on new experiences and insights.
- Evaluate how new influences or changes in your environment affect your overall alignment.

Note: Understand that alignment may require you to make adjustments as you grow and as your circumstances change. *Flexibility is key to maintaining long-term alignment.*

Part 4: Construct Your Path
Breaking Through Brick by Brick

By now, you've likely noticed that trauma is a core theme within the Meraki Journey franchise—and for good reason. Trauma can affect every aspect of our lives if we don't actively engage in the healing process. Left unresolved, it acts like invisible chains, holding us back from reaching our full potential. Whether we acknowledge it or push it deep down, the emotional scars we carry can shape our decisions, influence our beliefs, and trap us in cycles of stagnation.

So, how do we break free from these chains once and for all? How do we move past the trauma that keeps us stuck in areas of our lives where we long to grow? To truly liberate ourselves, we must transform our relationship with trauma itself.

Traditional approaches often focus on revisiting the pain in order to heal it. But the Meraki Journey offers a different path—one that reframes the entire narrative. Instead of being defined by our trauma, we learn to use it as a catalyst for growth and transformation.

Here are three powerful Meraki Journey Therapy approaches designed to help you do just that:

1. **Reconstructed Journaling**
2. **Somatic Healing**
3. **The Phoenix Method**

RECONSTRUCTED JOURNAL
Moving Past Mere Venting

Journaling is often praised as a means of self-expression, a way to unload our thoughts onto paper, and free our minds from being overwhelmed. While these are all true, the deeper questions remains:

- What happens next?
- Does journaling actually bring resolution or just a <u>momentary escape</u>?
- How can journaling move beyond mere venting, and actually lead to healing and growth?

This method goes beyond simply writing down our thoughts—it's about reshaping our narratives, empowering ourselves to reinterpret the past and reimagine our future. The key to transform journaling from a simple venting tool into a powerful instrument for healing lies in what we do <u>after</u> the words are written down.

Here's a little trick I taught myself over the years:

1. <u>Recognize the different selves within you:</u> The happy self, the angry self, the brave self, the intelligent self, and so on. Each has its own <u>voice</u> and <u>needs</u>.

2. <u>Determine which self is speaking as you write:</u> Is it the anxious one? The frustrated one? Whichever it is, allow that self to express fully, without holding back.

3. <u>Respect and honor that voice:</u> Let it speak its truth, without interruption or judgment.

4. Consider who should respond to this outpour: Which version of you is best suited to address what's been written? Perhaps the wise, the optimistic, the compassionate, or the rational one?

5. Embody that version of you: After some time—whether it's a day, a week, or a month—re-read your journal entry through this new lens. Respond directly to the version of you who initially wrote the entry.

Though the initial emotions that drove you to vent in your journal may still linger, this method allows you to access a fresh perspective. By inviting different versions of yourself to the table, you are gifting yourself with a new reality, and a renewed way of experiencing life—one that isn't **stuck in a single viewpoint**, but enriched by the diversity within you.

Self-Reflecting Questions

- **Has your perspective shifted?**
- **What new wisdom can you now offer yourself?**
- **How would you respond now to the situation?**

SOMATIC HEALING
Addressing the physical imprint of trauma.

When we think about the healing process from trauma, we often think about methods such as meditation, counselling, talk therapy, or journaling. However, trauma doesn't only affect us emotionally or psychologically. It can affect us physically as well. This means that even after doing the work to process our experiences mentally, the physical residue of trauma can remain—impacting our overall well-being.

Note: Our bodies can hold onto past traumas in ways that traditional talk therapy might not fully address.

Somatic healing techniques are designed to release any tension or pain that may have been stored in the muscles and tissues of the body for years, by calming the nervous system. Massages, acupuncture, and other physical therapies that help to release physical and emotional blockages are all considered to be somatic healing techniques. This technique not only alleviates the physical manifestations of trauma, but also supports emotional and psychological resilience.

Here are a few signs that somatic healing is missing from your healing journey:

- Tension in your neck or shoulders
- A tight jaw
- Lingering headaches
- Intense emotional responses
- Chronic fatigue
- Digestive issues

Unexplained Physical Aches and Pains: Recurring pain in certain areas of your body without a clear medical cause. These persistent aches could be your body's way of signaling that it's holding onto trauma.

Unexplained Chronic Fatigue: Exhaustion or a constant state of tiredness, despite getting enough rest. This type of fatigue is an overall weariness that no amount of rest seems to cure.

Emotional Reactivity: Heightened state of alertness is often a sign that your nervous system is stuck in survival mode. **1.** Overreacting to situations that wouldn't normally bother you. **2.** Triggered by certain places, sounds, or smells.

Unexplained Digestive Issues: Digestive issues like irritable bowel syndrome (IBS), nausea, or appetite changes that aren't linked to any dietary causes.

Note: Ever had "butterflies in your stomach" or a "gut feeling" about something? That's because our digestive system is incredibly sensitive to our emotional state.

THE PHOENIX METHOD
Unshackled By The Past

The Phoenix Method is a powerful, transformative approach to healing that guides you through a process of **release** and **rebirth**. Throughout this book, we've explored various ways to confront professional, emotional, spiritual, and personal stagnation. These sections were designed to help you to identify and release the mental, emotional, and behavioral barriers holding you back. Now, through the Phoenix Method, you will take all that you've learned, and use it to rise above the ashes of your past, and into a rebirth of your true self.

This method is not about forgetting or denying your past; it's about allowing your past experiences to become the fuel that ignites your growth. It's about transforming pain into power, and limitations into liberation. But most importantly, it's about shedding the labels and identities that no longer serve you and embracing a new, unshackled version of yourself.

A new version that thrives <u>because</u> of the trauma, not <u>in spite</u> of it. Meaning, The Phoenix Method allows us to surpass the need to *undo* the past. Instead we focus on crafting a self that embodies the lessons, resilience, and wisdom that our experiences has caused us to develop.

Believe it or not, I'm currently practicing this method myself.

It's a beautiful thing to thrive in spite of obstacles, but through self-reflecting, I've realized that I don't need to merely "make do" with the emotions and scars my past offered me. I asked myself: **Who am I today?** What do I want out of life? Not as a victim. Not as a survivor. Not even as a victor. And most certainly not as the product of trauma. But just as ME.

Imagine being born today as an adult, equipped with all the wisdom that you've gained, but free from the pressure to meet others' expectations. You'd be free. Free to create a life that aligns with what you truly want, not what your past demands of you. There would be no need to prove anything to anyone, and no reason to justify your worth to those who aren't willing or able to see it in the first place.

I'd need to remind myself that my worth isn't tied to how others see me, nor does it depend on overcoming some grand obstacle to prove I've triumphed over adversity. I'm simply living—not as a response to pain or a need to be better than my past self—but as the truest expression of who I desire to be.

So now, my question to you is: Who would you be? Who would you be if you weren't scarred by events of your past? Would you still struggle with trauma responses, gratitude guilt, or setting boundaries?

Note: Yes, trauma can happen at any stage of life, but that isn't the point. The real question still remains: **Who do you desire to be when you strip away the limitations that others—and even you—have placed on yourself?**

The Phoenix Method: Step-by-Step Guide
Meraki Journey Therapy Guide

> Imagine being born today, as an adult with the wisdom you've gathered but without the emotional weight of past traumas. Who would you be if you didn't have to carry the narrative of being a victim, a survivor, or even a victor? What kind of life would you create if you were free to choose your identity from scratch, based purely on your inner desires, untouched by the need for approval or validation?
>
> Upon answering the questions above, did you envision a specific life? ***If so, let's work on making that your reality.***

- ❖ The Phoenix Method is designed to lead you through a profound personal transformation by releasing the weight of past trauma, limiting beliefs, and external expectations.

- ❖ It combines elements of psychotherapy, self-help transformation, and mindfulness, to create a structured yet flexible path that anyone can follow.

Note: This method is deeply personal and highly adaptable to individual's unique needs.

Step 1: Self-Awareness – Acknowledging the Ashes
Building a foundation of self-awareness by recognizing and understanding the impact of past trauma or limiting experiences.

1. **Reflect on Your Past:** Spend time identifying specific experiences or traumas that have shaped your current beliefs, behaviors, and emotional responses. Use journaling, therapy sessions, or quiet introspection to surface these moments. Ask yourself:

   - What are major events that have impacted me emotionally, mentally, or spiritually?
   - How have these events influenced my view of myself and my life?

2. **Label and Name Your Emotions:** Rather than suppressing emotions, acknowledge them. Work on naming what you feel—anger, fear, shame, guilt, sadness, etc. This helps create distance between you and your emotions, making it easier to work with them.

<u>**Practice the emotional awareness techniques.**</u> *Please refer to your **Navigating Stagnation:** Strategic Journaling for further breakdown.*

3. **Seek Clarity:** Now that you've acknowledged your past, look for the patterns. Are there recurring themes? What negative beliefs or behaviors have you carried forward? Identifying these patterns will help you determine what needs to be released.

<u>**Example:**</u> "I tend to withdraw in relationships because I fear abandonment, a pattern that stems from my childhood."

Step 2: Release – Burning Through the Pain
Confront and release the emotional weight of your past, shedding the old layers that no longer serve you.

1. **Engage in Therapy or Support Systems:** Seek professional help or join support groups that allow you to safely express and process your trauma. Cognitive-behavioral therapy (CBT), somatic therapy, or trauma-focused therapy are ideally effective.

Example: Working with a therapist to reframe the negative beliefs formed during traumatic experiences. Such as: "I'm not good enough" and replacing them with healthier beliefs.

2. **Forgive Yourself and Others:** Forgiveness doesn't mean excusing harmful behavior; it's about letting go of the grip it has on you. Write letters (even if unsent), or engage in forgiveness exercises that help you release resentment or guilt.

3. **Use Active Methods of Release:** Engage in activities that symbolize release—burn old letters, or engage in high intensity activities like running or kickboxing. This can represent the act of breaking through barriers.

Example: Write down the things that hold you back and burn the paper, symbolizing the end of those emotional chains.

Step 3: Rebirth – Reimagining Your Identity
Redefine yourself beyond your trauma, external pressures, and limiting beliefs by embracing the person you truly desire to be.

Please find the remaining of **The Phoenix Method: Step-by-Step Guide** in your "**Navigating Stagnation: Strategic Journaling**" journal.

As you continue this journey, remember that it's not about perfection. It's about allowing yourself to live authentically, free from the chains of your past and the expectations of others.

Shattered Perception
By: Crystal Hamilton

My name is Crystal. For five long years, I endured an abusive relationship that left deep scars on my soul. Although it's been over a year since I walked away, the trauma lingers like an unwelcomed shadow. Even though I recognized the need to heal, the effects of that past relationship have made trusting others—especially in romantic contexts—an excruciatingly difficult challenge. I want love and companionship more than anything, yet the fear of being hurt again is keeping me from opening up. This fear isn't limited to romance; it extends to all relationships, causing me to keep people at a distance, even in the most platonic of connections. It's a cruel irony that while I craved closeness, the pain of past betrayals made me retreat into emotional isolation.

For over a year, I found myself stuck in a cycle of unfulfilling situations. Love had become a source of anxiety rather than joy. The aftermath of the volatile breakup often triggered me into a pattern of isolating myself whenever I sensed emotional vulnerability. Despite my desperate yearning for happiness, the echoes of past abuse left me feeling paralyzed, and unable to fully accept those who wanted to genuinely care for me. My experiences have distorted my self-image, instilling deep feelings of unworthiness and guilt, making me believe that I somehow deserved the mistreatment. This pervasive self-doubt and negative self-talk have trapped me in a cycle of trauma, making it hard to move forward.

I've noticed how I avoid situations or people that might remind me of the abuse, unintentionally narrowing my chances for personal growth and meaningful connections. Although I may appear strong and resilient on the outside, internally, I feel ensnared by the weight of my past, struggling to fully embrace the present or envision a future unburdened by old wounds.

Through therapy, I am slowly learning to navigate these challenges. I'm acquiring tools to cope with my past, questioning and reshaping negative thought patterns, and beginning to restore my sense of self-worth and trust. It's a gradual process, but with ongoing effort and support, I am starting to rewrite my narrative. I am reclaiming my power and embarking on a journey of healing and self-discovery, moving closer to a future where I can embrace love and connection once again.

Thank you Dr. Baker for giving me this opportunity to tell my story.

-Crystal Hamilton

Closing: The Journey to Becoming Whole

As I sit here, reflecting on the words that fill this book, I am reminded of one fundamental truth. *The journey to healing is not about arriving at a perfect, unscarred version of ourselves.* It's about recognizing that we are already whole, even as we continue to grow, evolve, and shed the layers of our past. The scars we bear, the traumas we've experienced, and the emotions we've carried—none of these define our worth or our future.

In writing this book, I wanted to share not just a narrative of overcoming, but a deeper invitation. *An invitation to break free from the belief that healing is the ultimate goal.* Instead, what if we saw our lives as an ongoing process of <u>becoming</u>? A process not bound by our history or our traumas, but rather propelled by the lessons we've learned along the way. This is the essence of the Phoenix Method: to rise, not in spite of our past, but because of it, using it as the fuel for our evolution.

Always remember: we are not here to undo the past, we are here to build a future.

Embracing Wholeness: Wholeness isn't about perfection; it's about embracing the totality of who you are—your light, your shadows, your successes, and your failures. When we stop searching for healing as a way to erase our wounds, we can see ourselves clearly. We can see that our strength comes not from having overcome, it comes from the quiet moments when we choose to live in the present, rather than be trapped by the pain of the past.

AUTHOR'S MESSAGE

I hope that beautiful things happen to you. And when they do, I hope that you believe that you are worthy of every single one of them. No matter where you've been, or what you've faced, you are deserving of the love, care, and growth you seek.

Remember: Be gentle with yourself along the way. Take your time, breathe deeply, and know that you are never alone in this journey. I believe in you, and I pray for God's blessings of abundance, fruitfulness, and multiplication to remain a part of your inheritance now and forevermore.

With love and light,

Dr. Christina Baker

Made in the USA
Middletown, DE
16 February 2025